Ingres:

106 Masterpieces

By Maria Tsaneva

First Edition

*****

Ingres: 107 Paintings and Drawings
*****

Foreword

Jean-Auguste-Dominique Ingres (1780 –1867) was a French Neoclassical painter. Although he considered himself to be a painter of history in the tradition of Nicolas Poussin and Jacques-Louis David, by the end of his life it was Ingres's portraits, both painted and drawn, that were recognized as his greatest legacy.

A man profoundly respectful of the past, he assumed the role of a guardian of academic orthodoxy against the ascendant Romantic style represented by his nemesis Eugène Delacroix. His exemplars, he once explained, were "the great masters which flourished in that century of glorious memory when Raphael set the eternal and incontestable bounds of the sublime in art ... I am thus a conservator of good doctrine, and not an innovator." Nevertheless, modern opinion has tended to regard Ingres and the other Neoclassicists of his era as embodying the Romantic spirit of his time, while his expressive distortions of form and space make him an important precursor of modern art.

Ingres is the son of a minor painter and sculptor, Jean-Marie-Joseph Ingres (1755-1814). After an early academic training in the Toulouse Academy he went to Paris in 1796 and was a fellow student of Gros in David's studio. He won the Prix de Rome in 1801, but owing to the state of France's economy he was not awarded the usual stay in Rome until 1807. In the interval he produced his first portraits. These fall into two categories: portraits of himself and his friends, conceived in a Romantic spirit (Self-portrait, 1804), and portraits of well-to-do clients characterized by purity of line and enamel-like colouring. These early portraits are notable for their calligraphic line and expressive contour, which had a sensuous beauty of its own beyond its function to contain and delineate form. It was a feature that formed the essential basis of Ingres's painting throughout his life.

During his first years in Rome he continued to execute portraits and began to paint bathers, a theme which was to become one of his favourites. He remained in Rome when his four-year scholarship ended, earning his living principally by pencil portraits of members of the French colony. But he also received more substantial commissions, including two decorative paintings for Napoleon's palace in Rome. In 1820 he moved from Rome to Florence, where he remained for 4 years, working mainly on his Raphaelesque Vow of Louis XIII, commissioned for the cathedral of Montauban.

Ingres's work had often been severely criticized in Paris because of its 'Gothic' distortions, and when he accompanied this painting to the Salon of 1824 he was surprised to find it acclaimed and himself set up as the leader of the academic opposition to the new Romanticism. Ingres stayed in Paris for the next ten years and received the official success and honours he had always craved. During this period he devoted much of his time to executing two large works: The Apotheosis of Homer, for a ceiling in the Louvre, and The Martyrdom of St Symphorian (1834) for the cathedral of Autun. When the latter painting was badly received, however, he accepted the Directorship of the French School in Rome, a post he retained for 7 years. He was a model administrator and teacher, greatly improving the school's facilities, but he produced few major works in this period.

In 1841 he returned to France, once again acclaimed as the champion of traditional values. He was heartbroken when his wife died in 1849, but he made a happy second marriage in 1852, and he continued working with great energy into his 80s. One of his acknowledged masterpieces, the extraordinarily sensuous Turkish Bath dates from the last years of his life. At his death he left a huge bequest of his work (several paintings and more than 4,000 drawings) to his home town of Montauban.

Ingres is a puzzling artist and his career is full of contradictions. Yet more than most artists he was obsessed by a restricted number of themes and returned to the same subject again and again over a long period of years. He was a bourgeois with the limitations of a bourgeois mentality but as Baudelaire remarked, his finest works 'are the product of a deeply sensuous nature'. The central contradiction of his career is that although he was held up as the guardian of classical rules and precepts, it is his personal obsessions and mannerisms that make him such a great artist. His technique as a painter was academically unimpeachable.

Paintings and Drawings

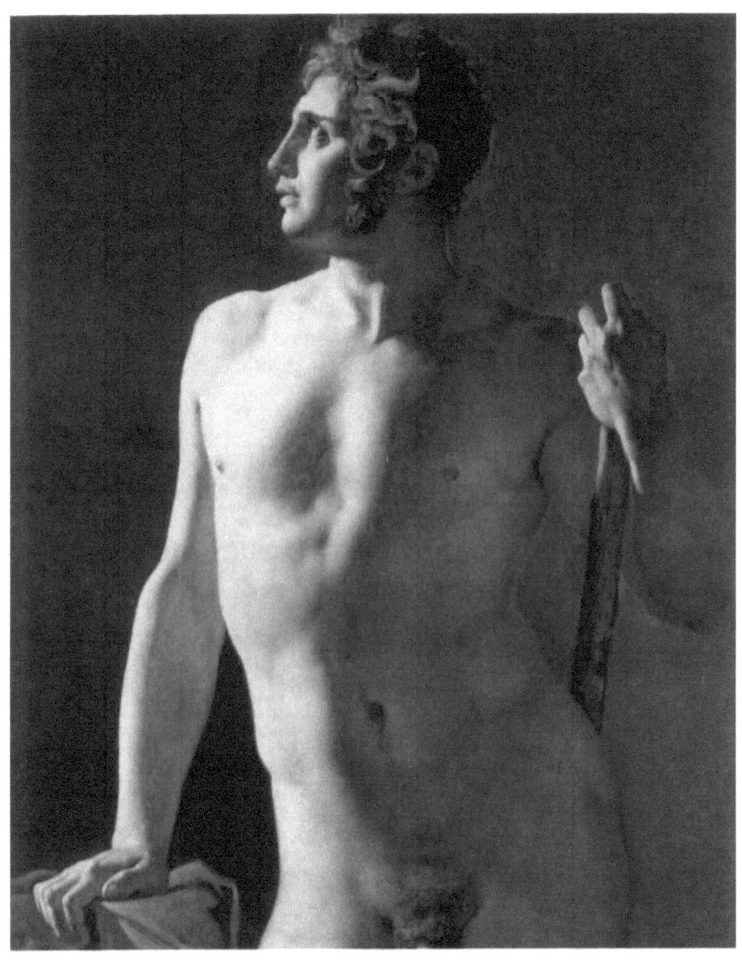

Male Torso, 1800, oil on canvas

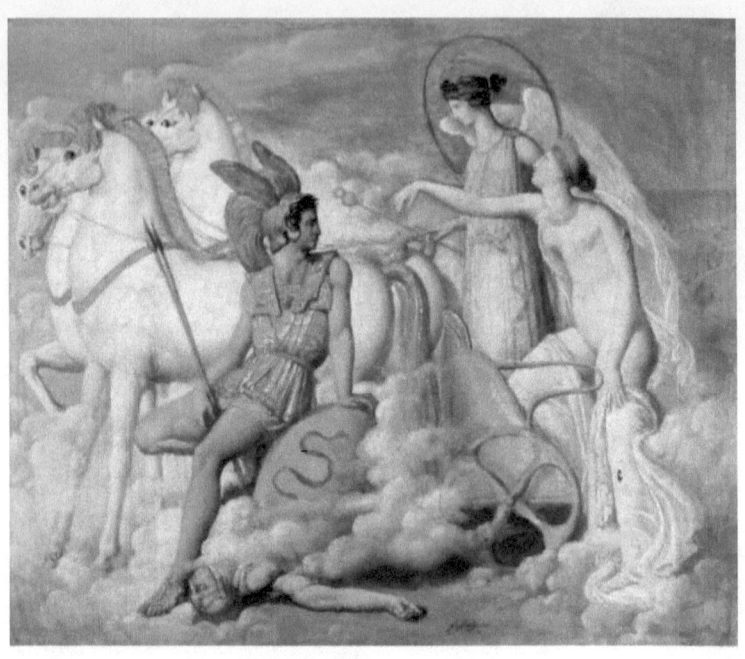

Venus, Wounded by Diomedes, Returns to Olympus,
1800, oil on canvas

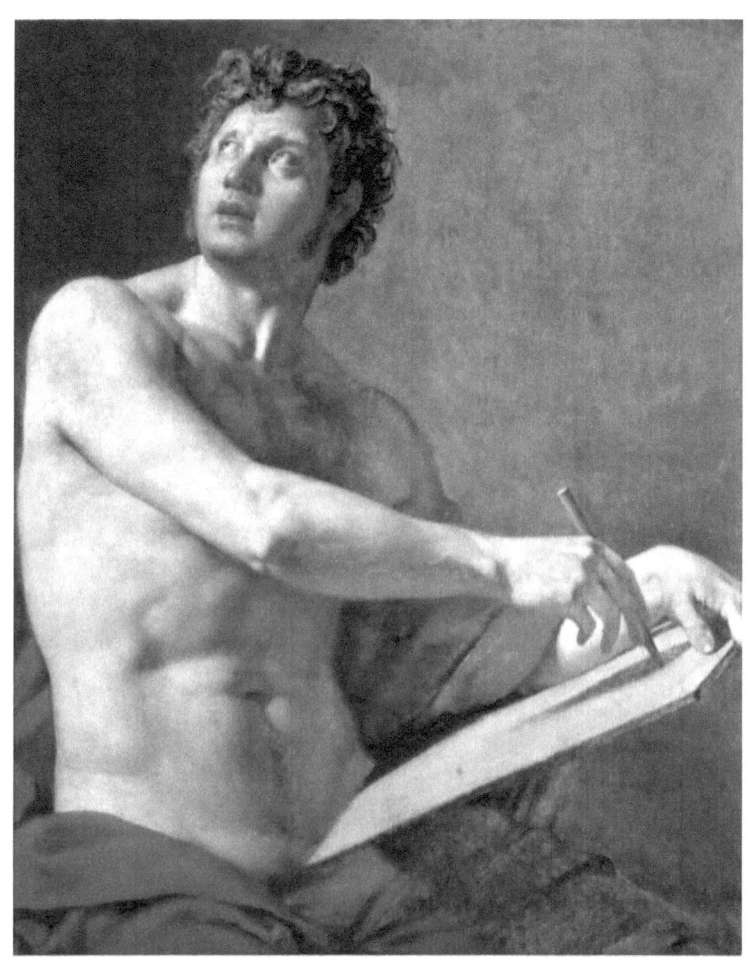

Academic Study of a Male Torse, 1801, oil on canvas

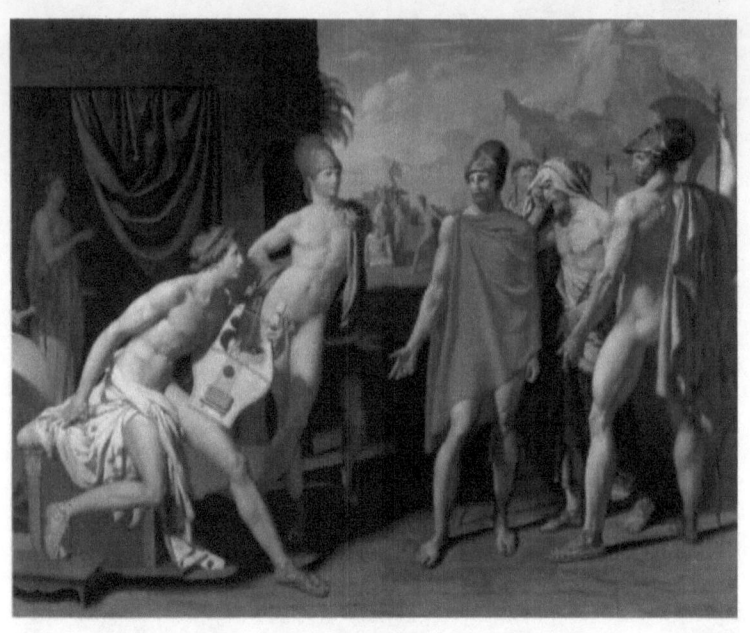

Ambassadors Sent by Agamemnon to Urge Achilles to
Fight, 1801, oil on panel

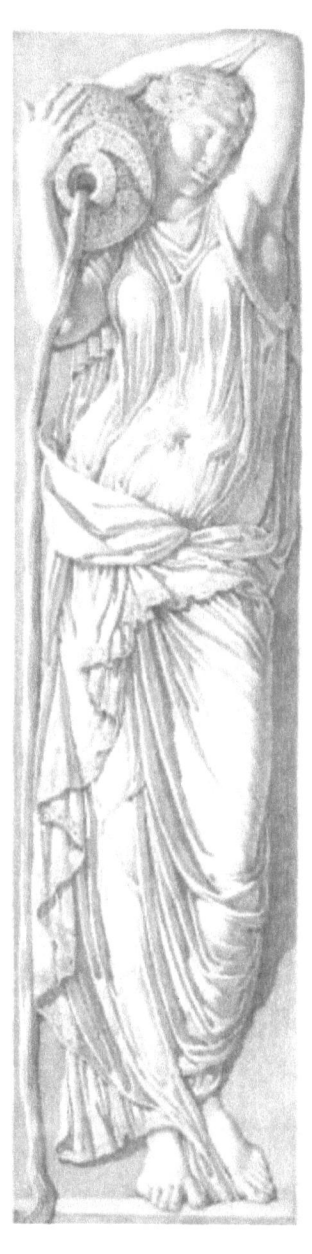

A nymph (after Jean Goujon), 1802-1806, graphite on
paper

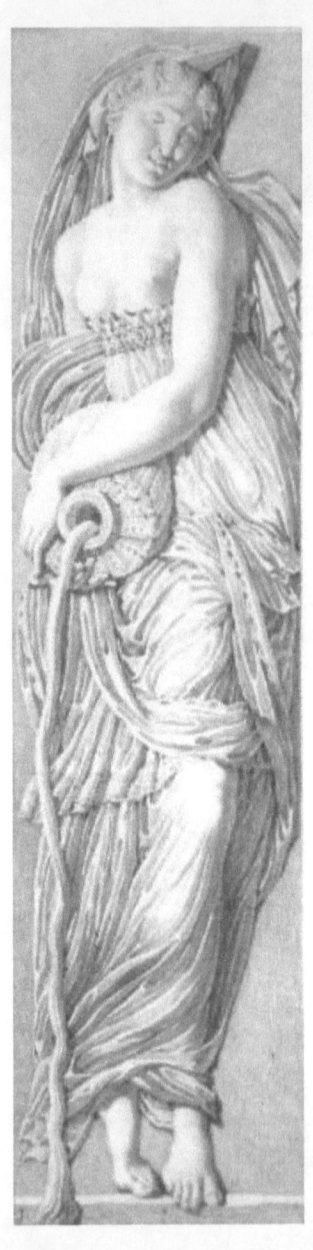

A nymph (after Jean Goujon), 1802-1806, graphite on paper

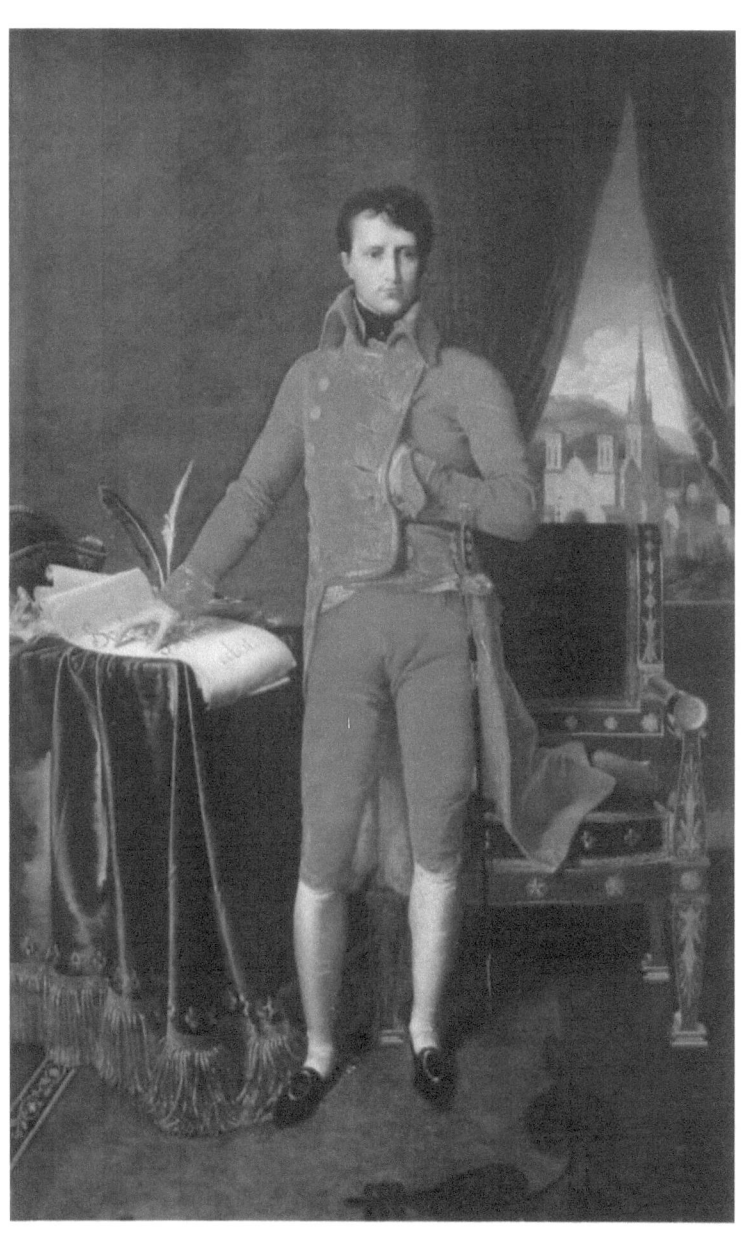

Portrait of Napoléon Bonaparte, The First Council,
1804, oil on canvas

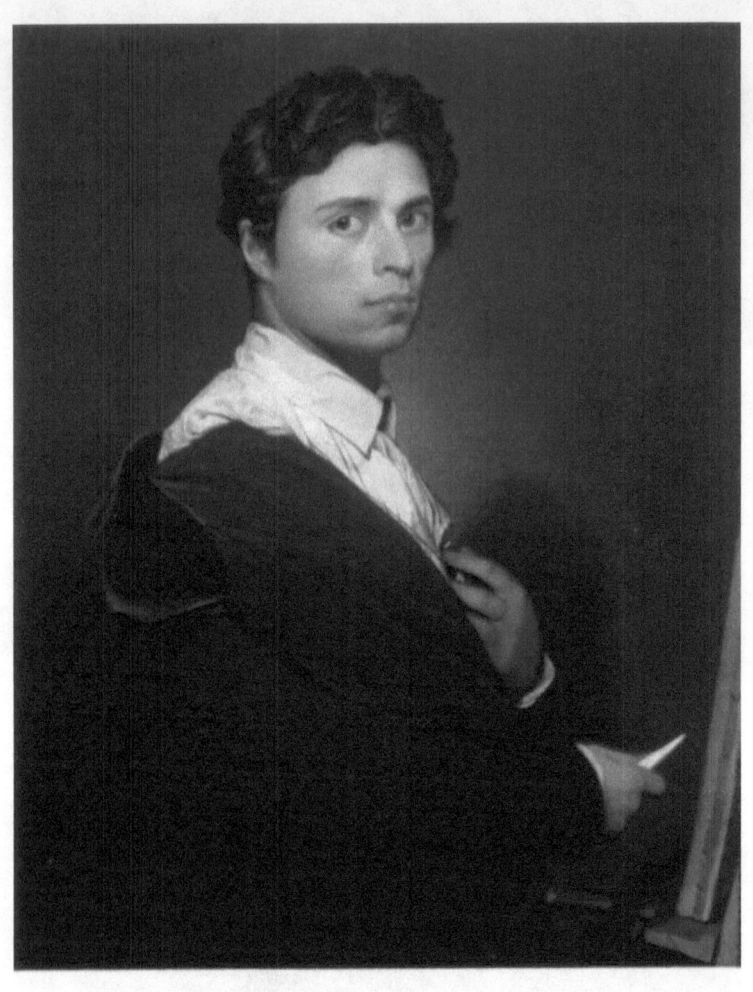

Self-Portrait at the Age of 24, 1804, oil on canvas

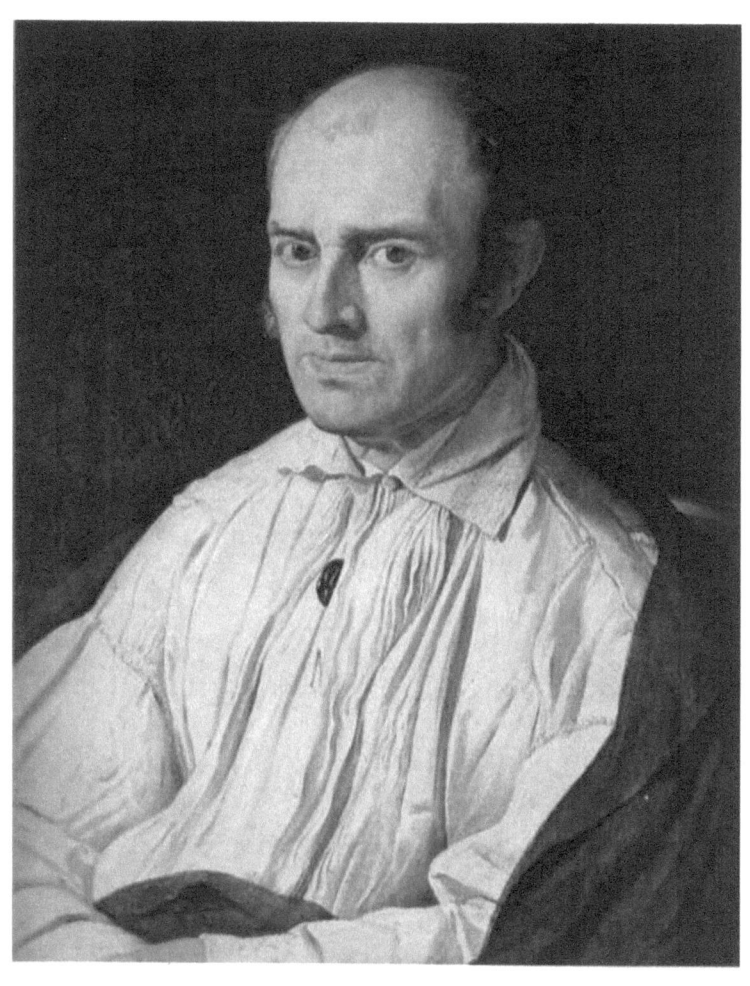

Portrait of Frédéric Desmarais, 1805, oil on canvas

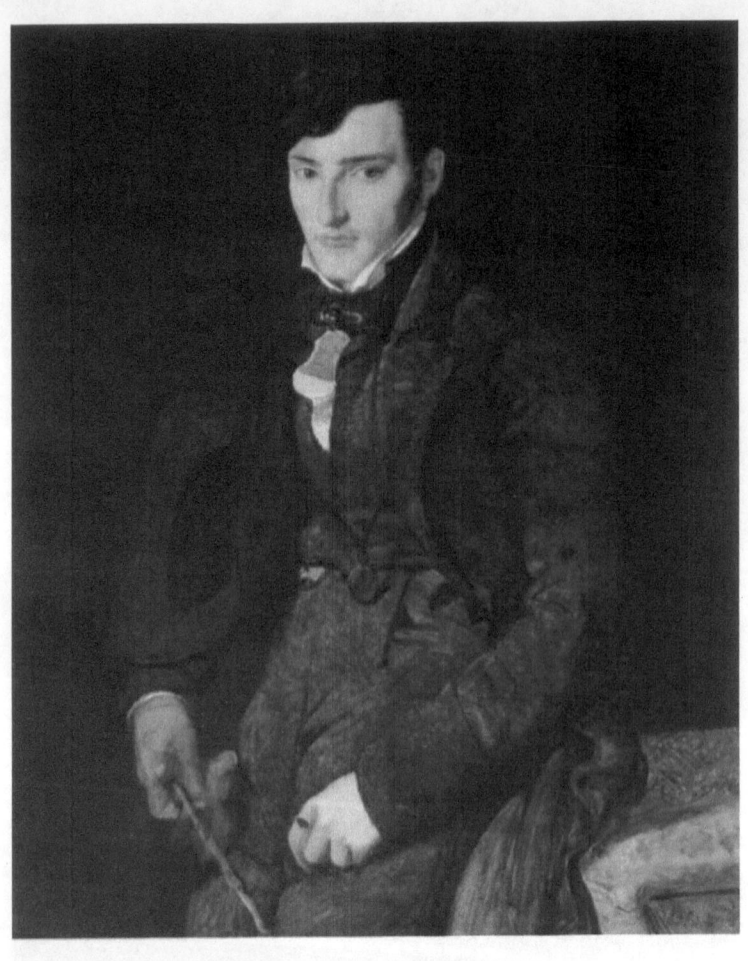

Portrait of Jean-Pierre-Francois Gilibert, 1804-1805, oil on canvas

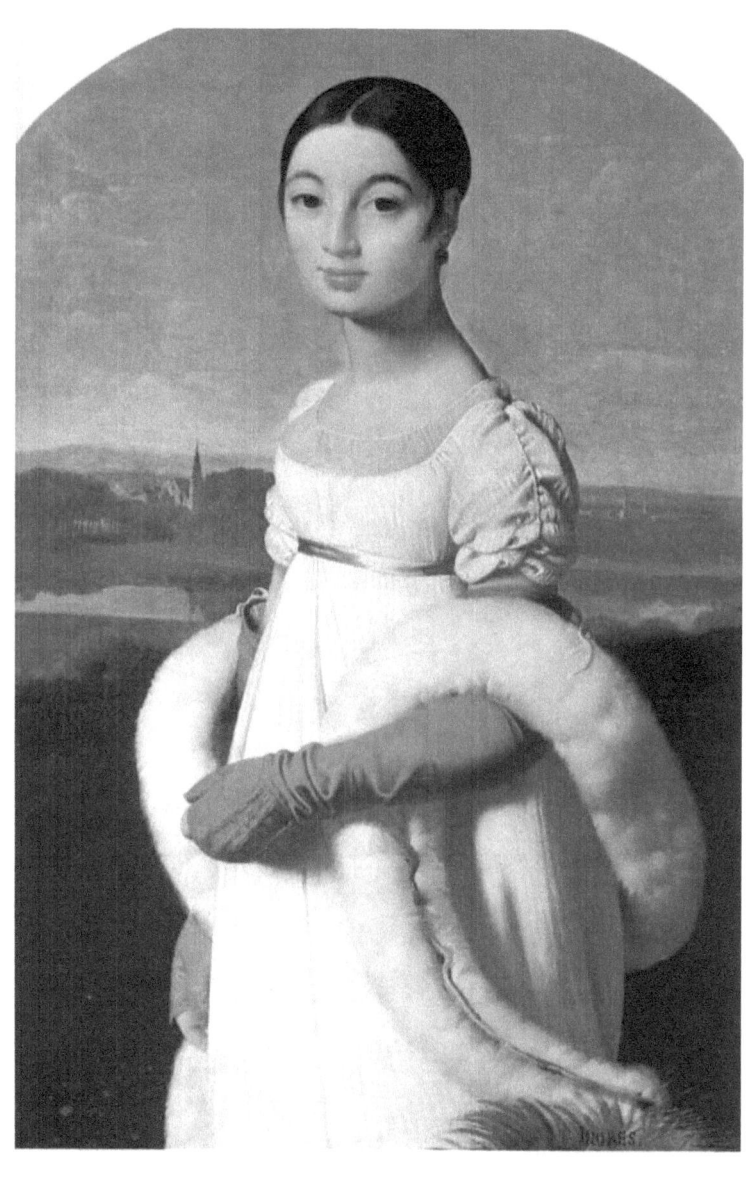

Portrait of Mademoiselle Rivière, 1805, oil on canvas

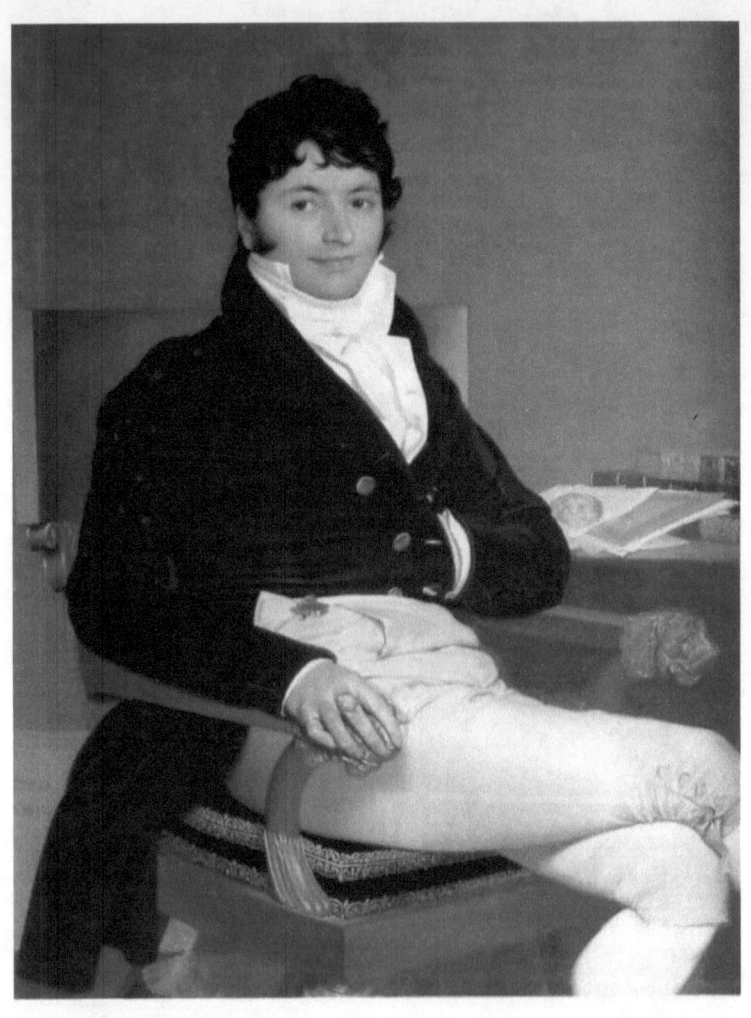

Portrait of Monsieur Rivière, 1805, oil on canvas

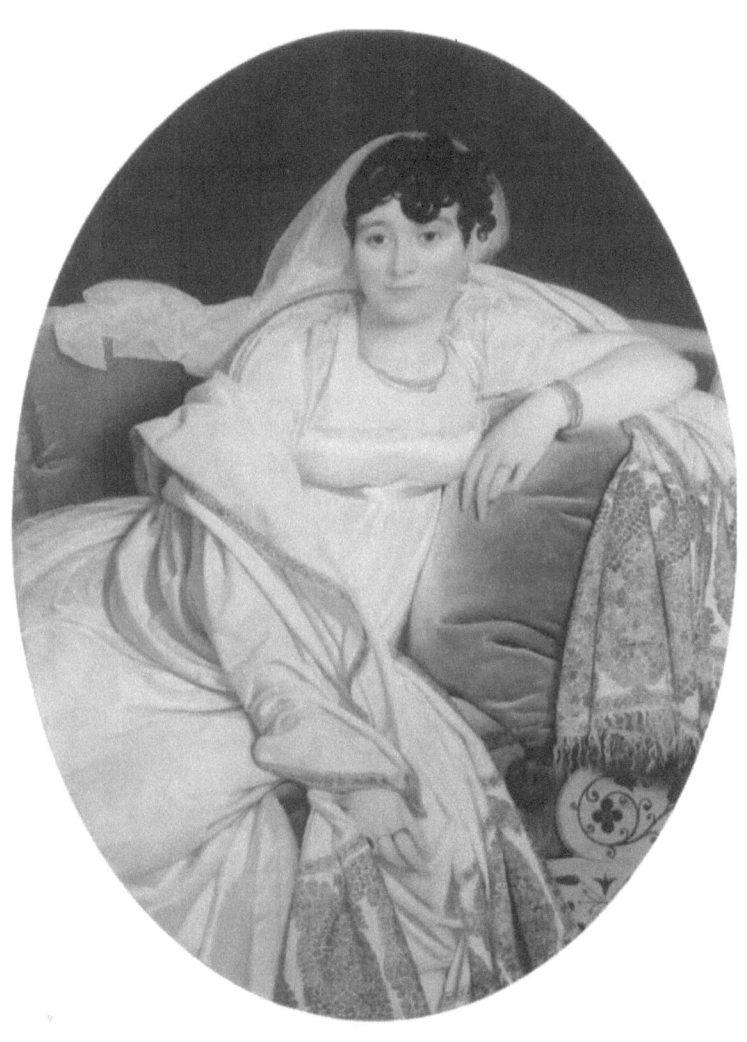

Portrait of Madame Riviere nee Marie Francoise Jacquette Bibiane Blot de Beauregard, 1806, oil on canvas

The portrait of Madame Riviere, née Marie Francoise Jacquette Bibiane Blot de Beauregard (1773/74 - 1848) was exhibited at the Salon of 1806, together with the portraits of Monsieur Riviere and their daughter. These portraits show the influence of Raphael and other Florentine painters.

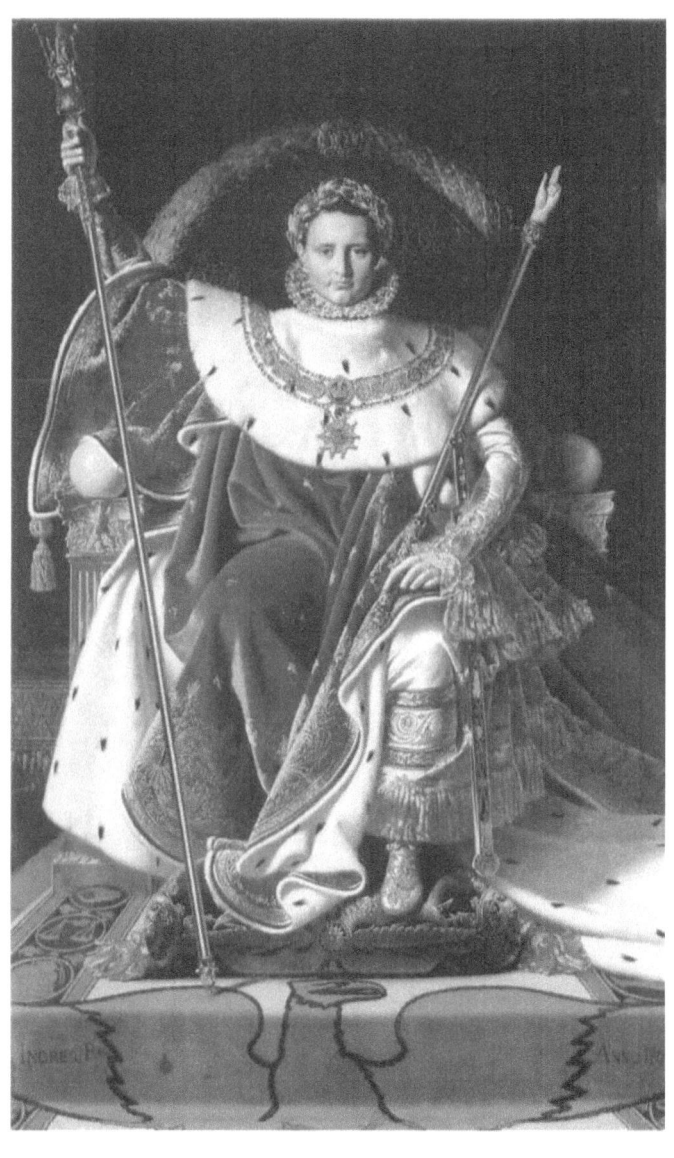

Portrait of Napoléon on the Imperial Throne, 1806, oil on canvas

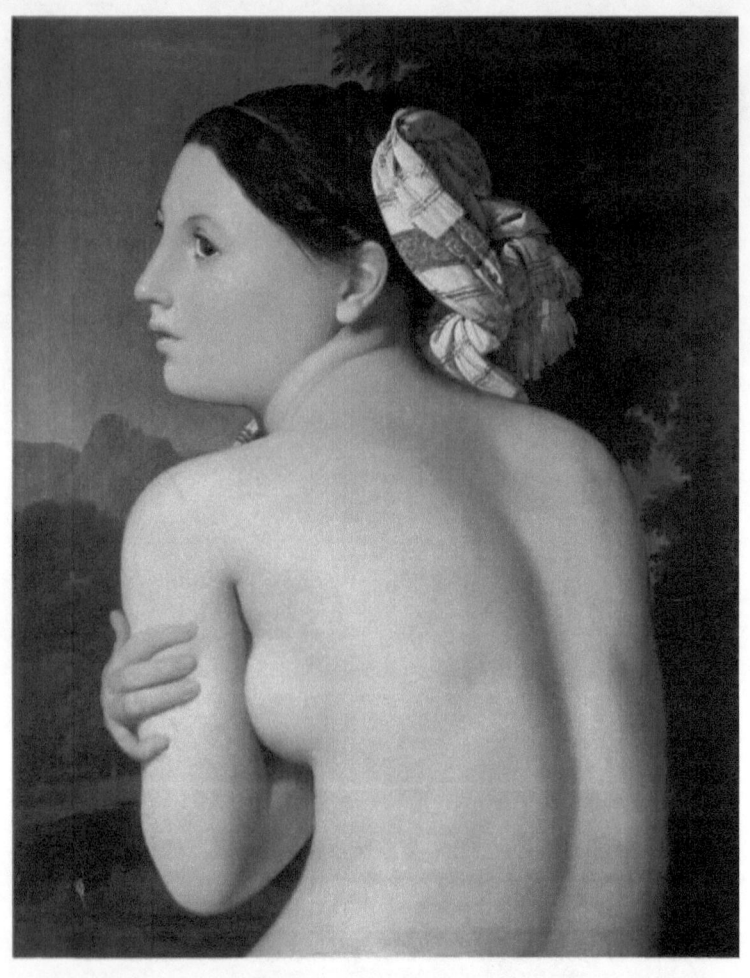

Half-figure of a Bather, 1807, oil on canvas

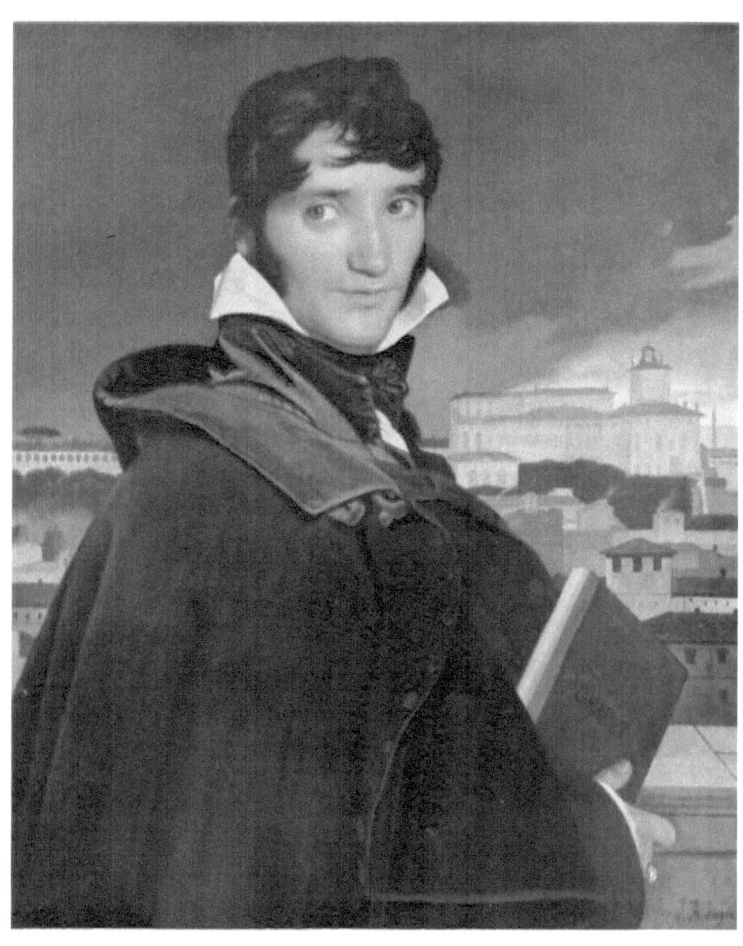

Portrait of Francois-Marius Granet, 1807, oil on canvas

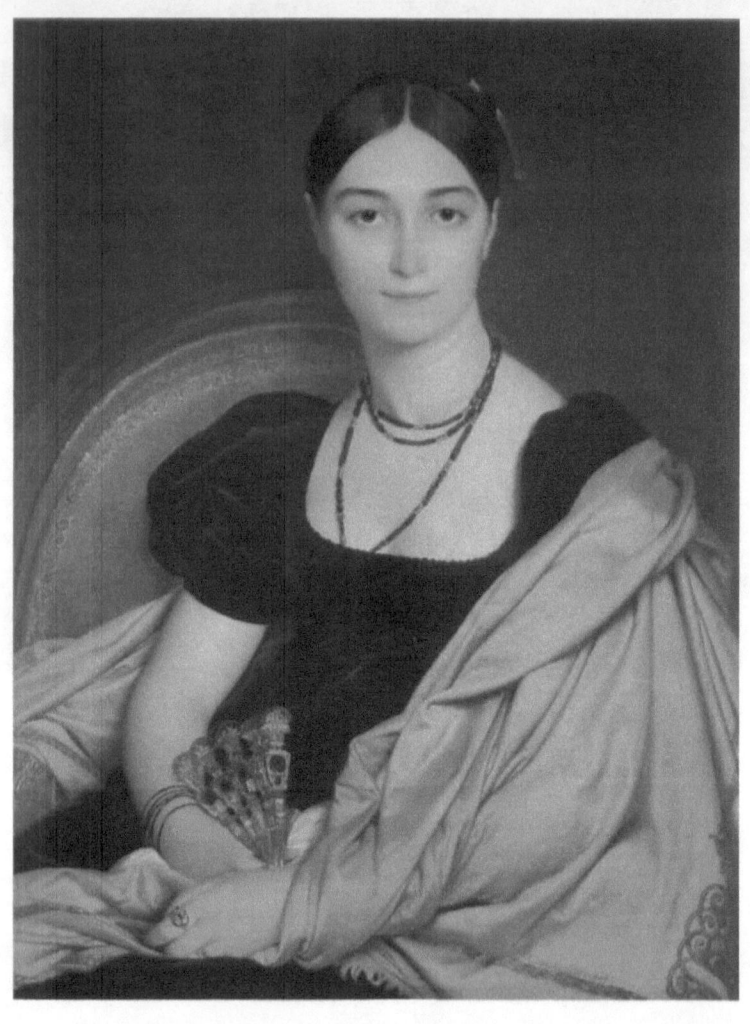

Portrait of Madame Antonia de Vaucay nee de Nittis,
1807, oil on canvas

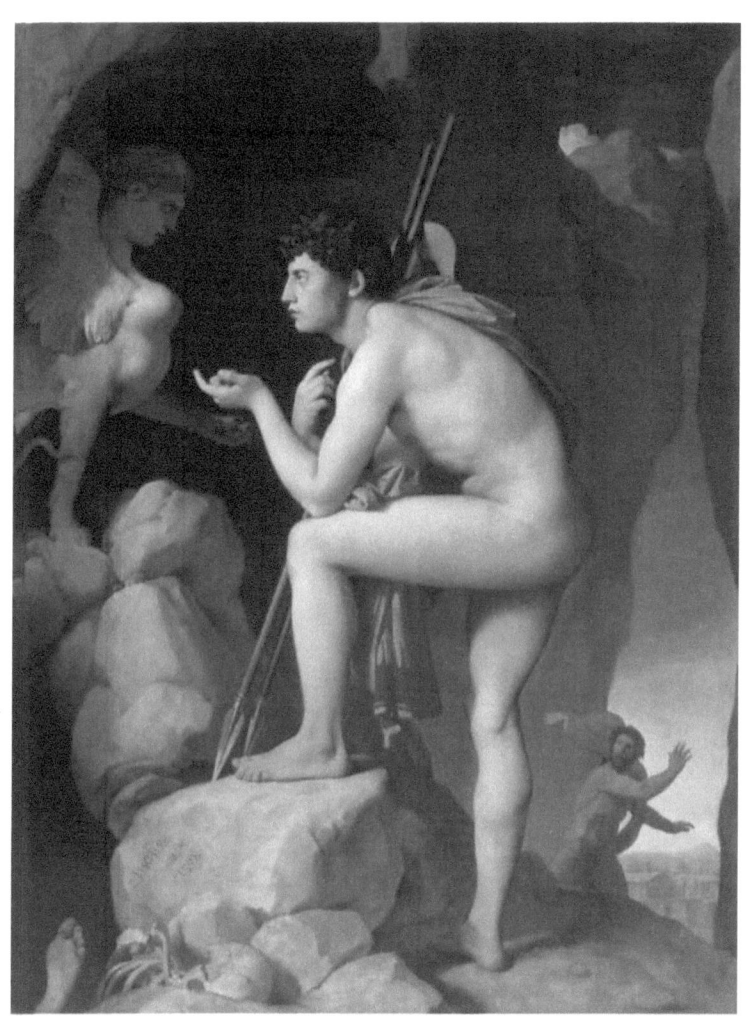

Oedipus and the Sphinx, 1808-1825, oil on canvas

According to the classic myth, as rendered in Sophocles' Oedipus Rex, Oedipus came to the Sphynx, who blocked the road to Thebes and challenged every traveler to answer a riddle or die. Oedipus mastered the riddle and the Sphynx jumped to her death in mortification. Ingres first painted this composition in 1808, then changed it before presenting it at the Salon of 1827.

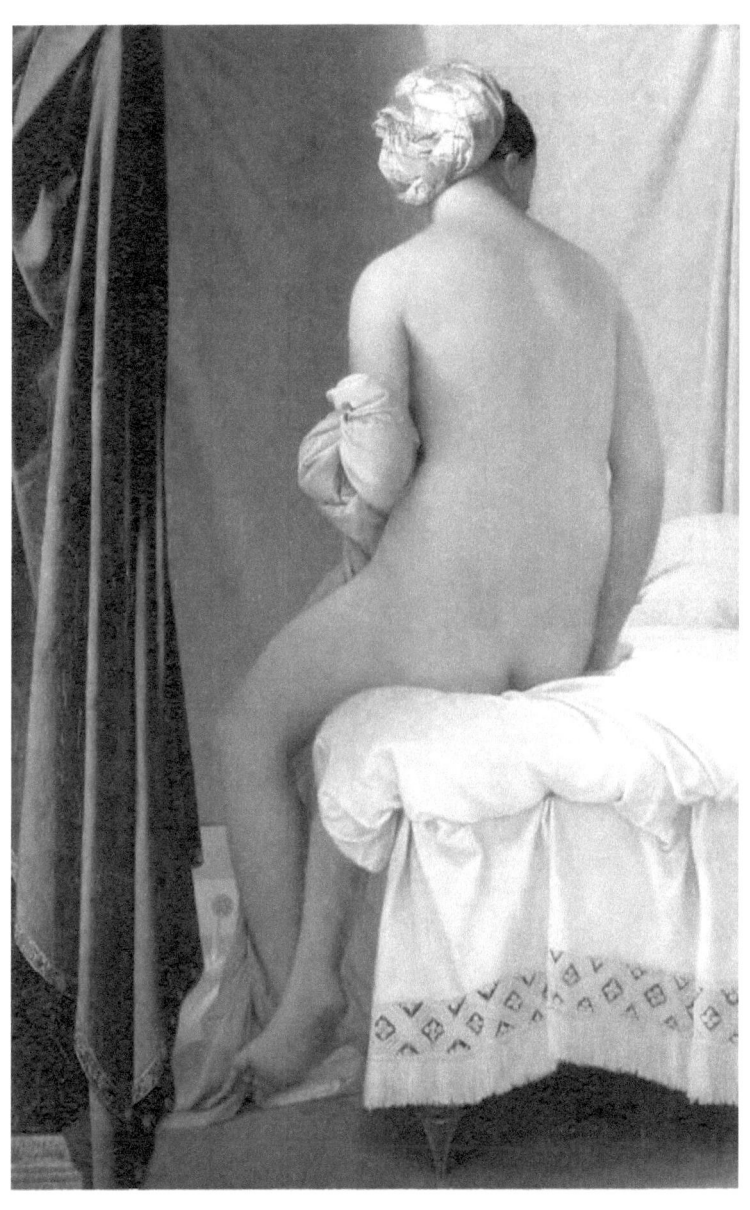

The Bather of Valpinçon, 1808, oil on canvas

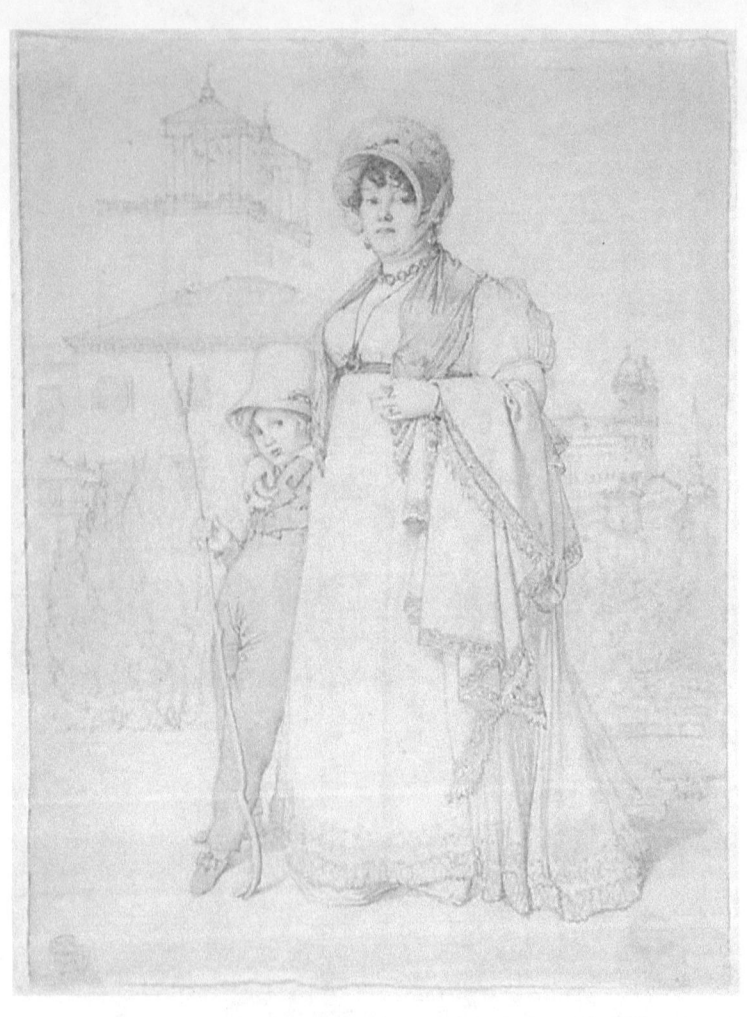

Madame Guillaume Guillon Lethière, née Marie-
Joseph-Honorée Vanzenne, and her son Lucien
Lethière, 1808, Graphite

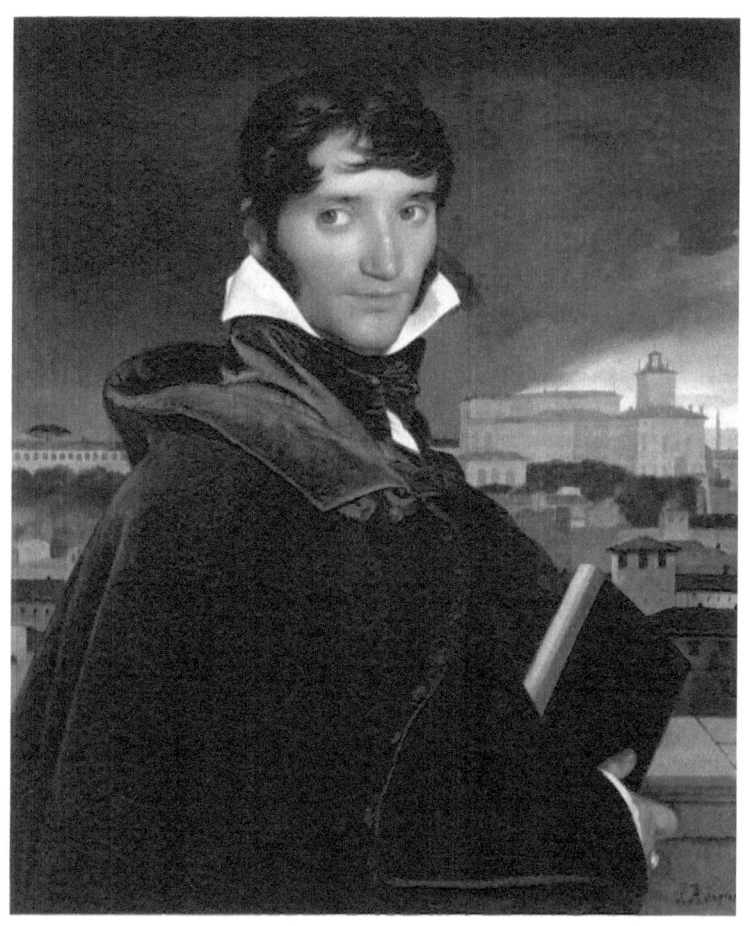

The painter Francois-Marius Granet enjoyed great success for his historical and interior scenes. In this painting he himself is the subject of one of the most intensely Romantic of all artists' portraits, painted by his friend Ingres.

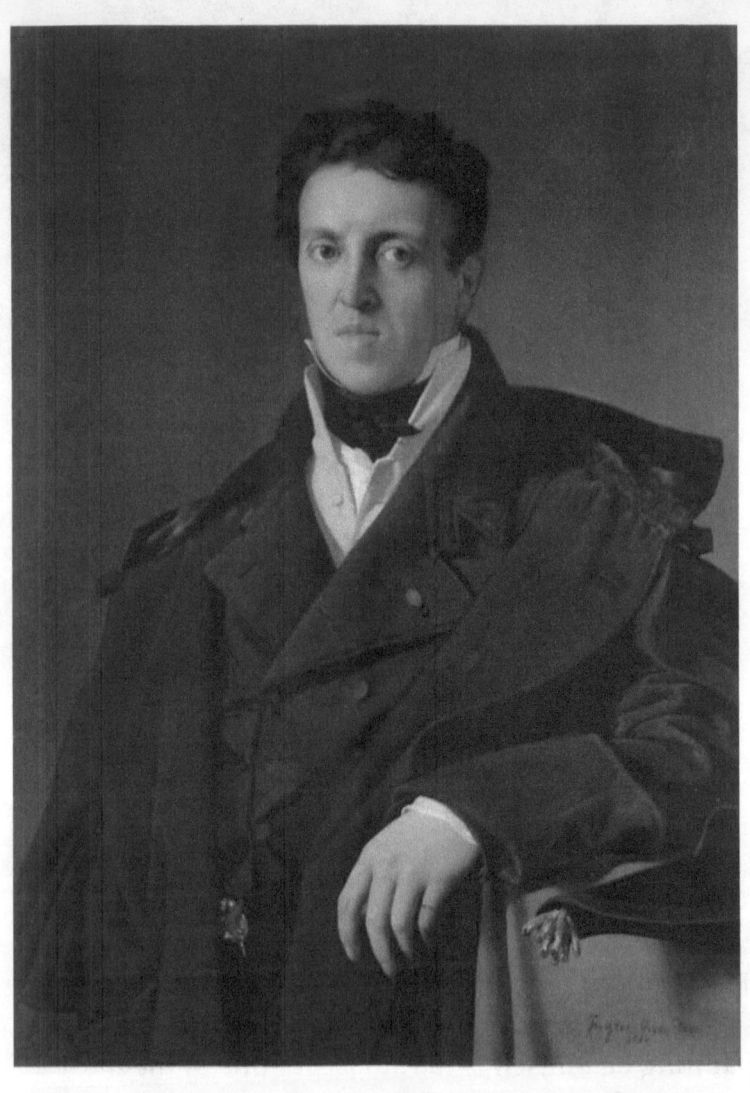

Charles-Marie-Jean-Baptiste Marcotte (Marcotte d'Argenteuil), 1810, oil on canvas

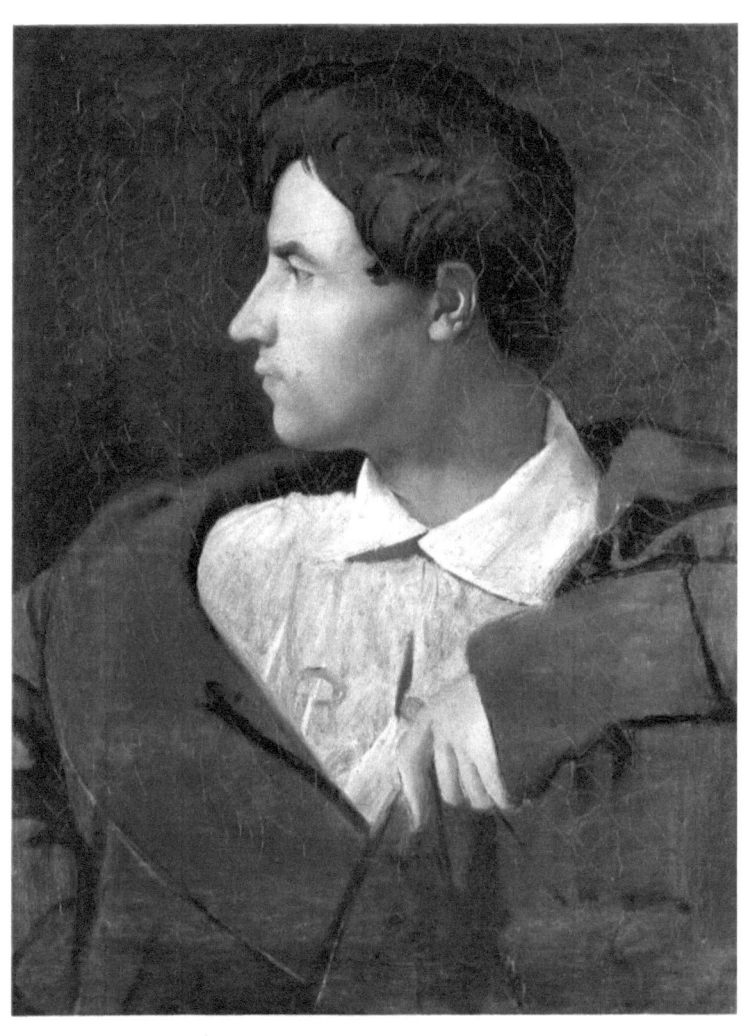

Jean Baptiste Desdeban, 1810, oil on canvas

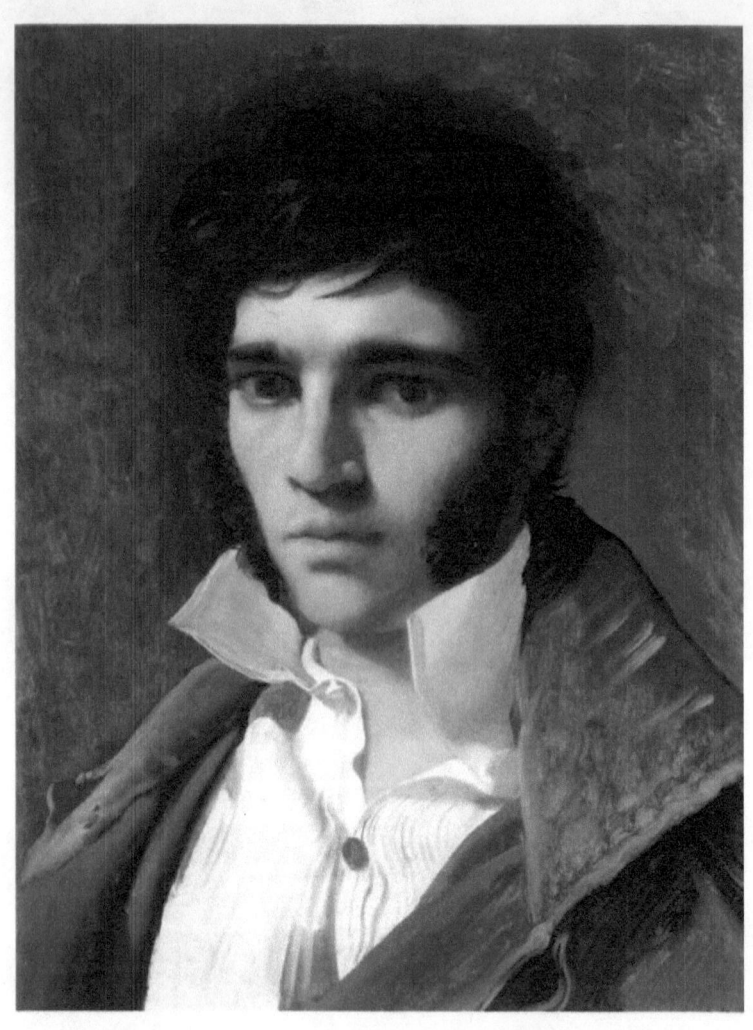

Paul Lemoyne, 1810, oil on canvas

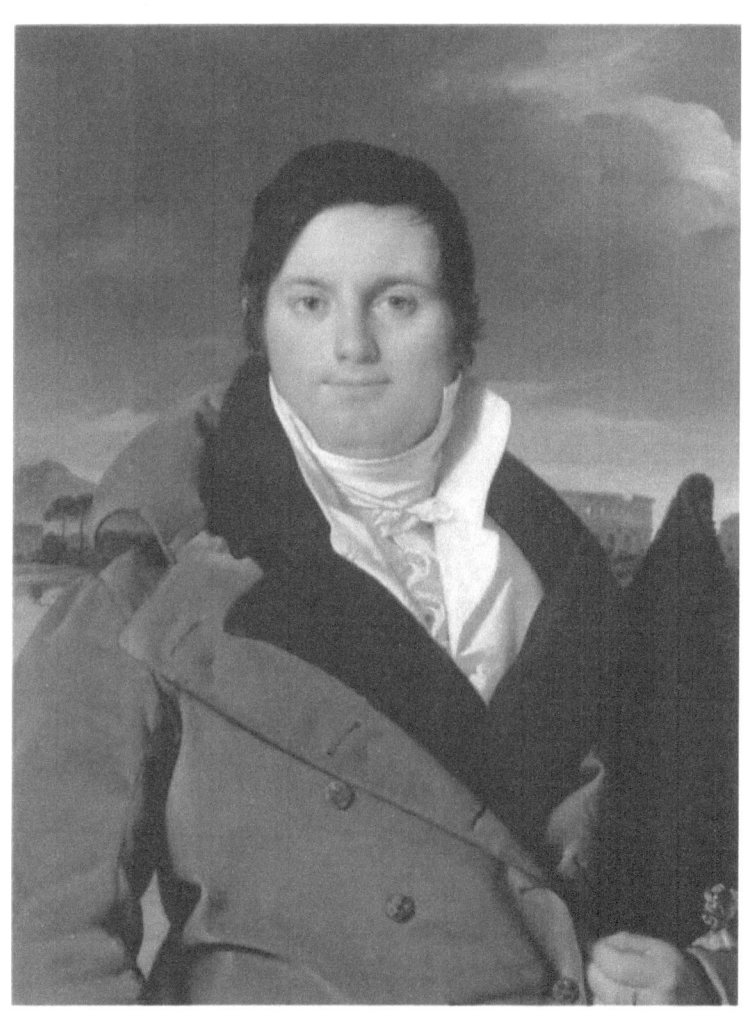

Portrait of Joseph-Antoine Moltedo, c.1810, oil on canvas

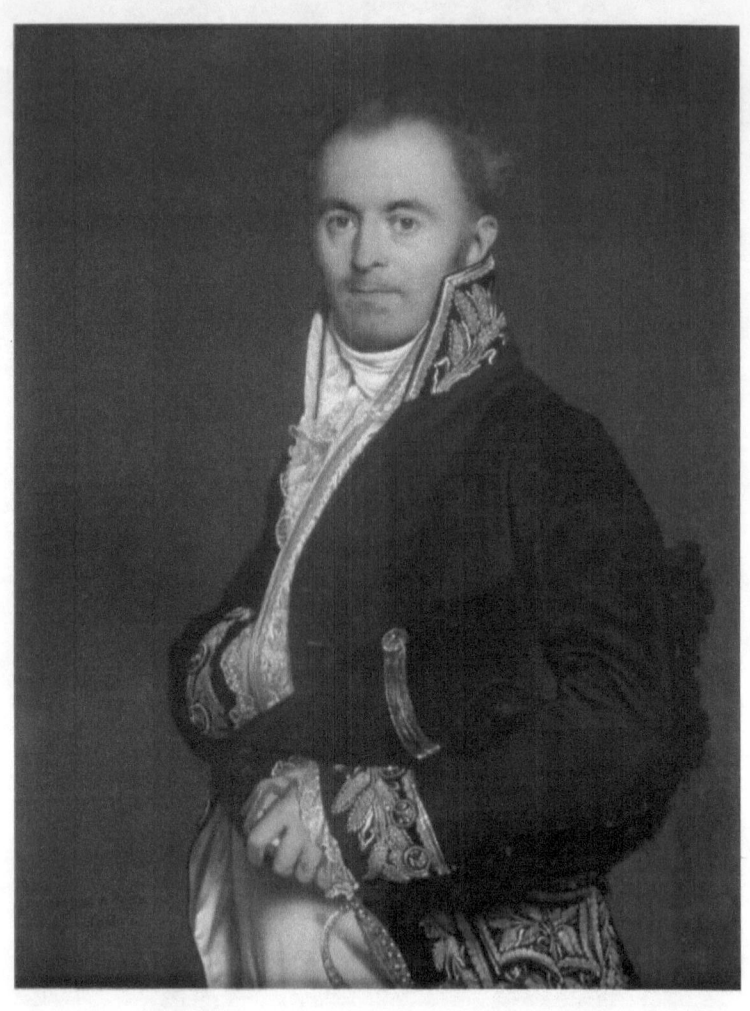

Hippolyte-François Devillers, 1811, oil on canvas

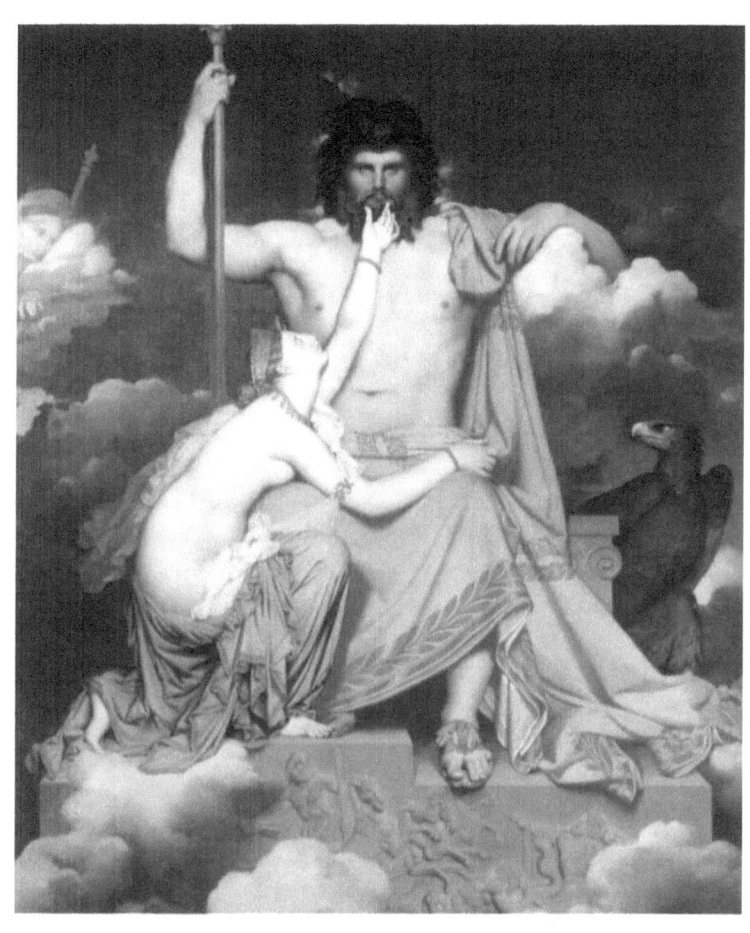

Jupiter and Thetis, 1811, oil on canvas

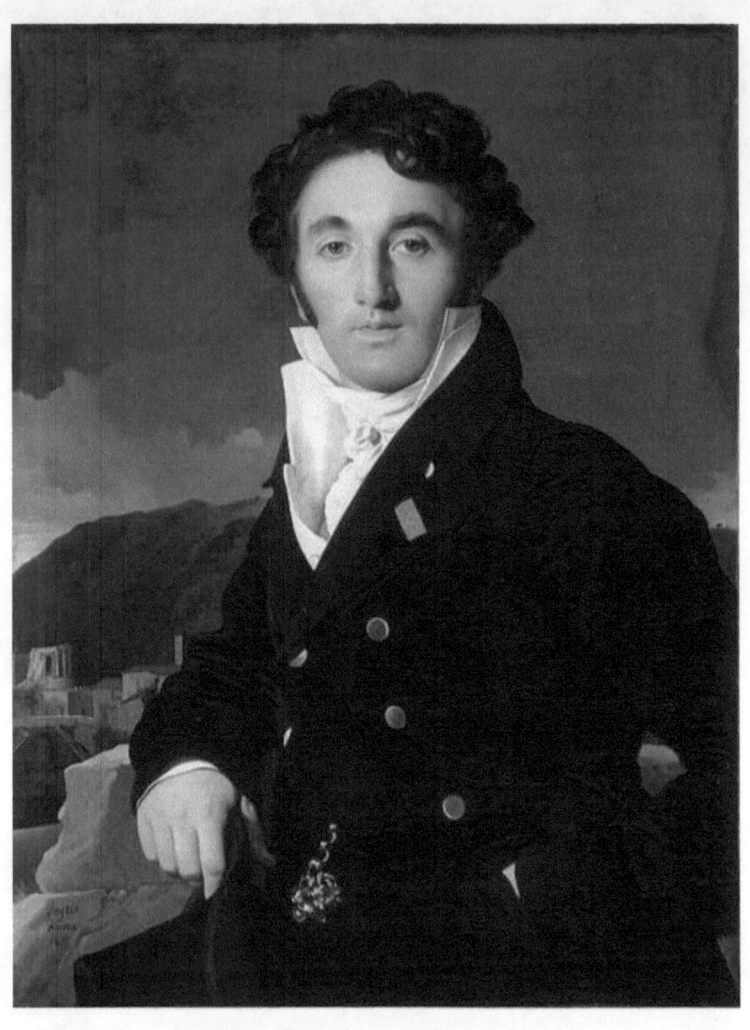

Portrait of Charles-Joseph-Laurent Cordier, 1811, oil on canvas

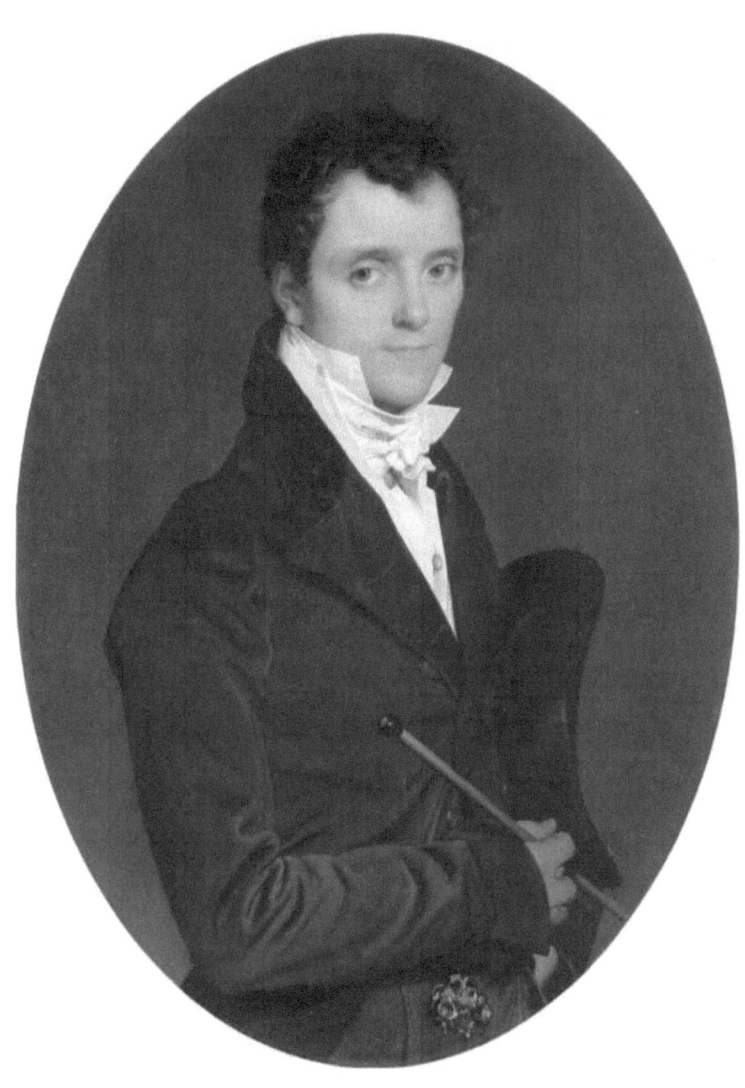

Portrait of Edme Bochet, 1811, oil on canvas

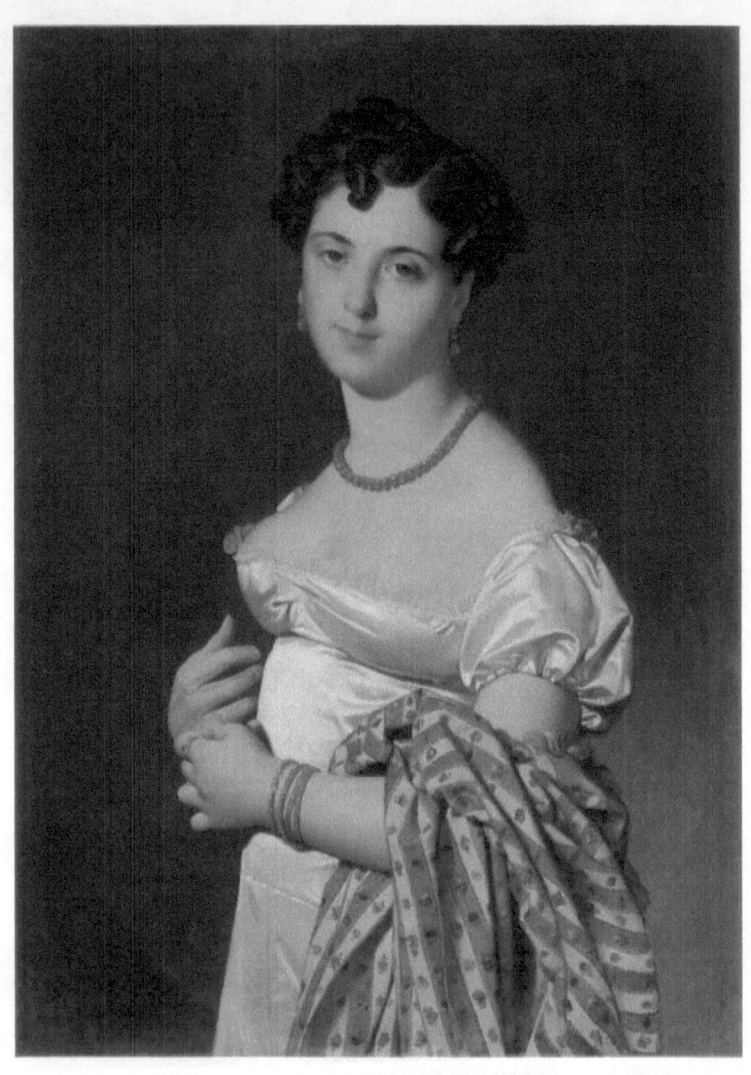

Portrait of Madame Panckoucke, 1811, oil on canvas

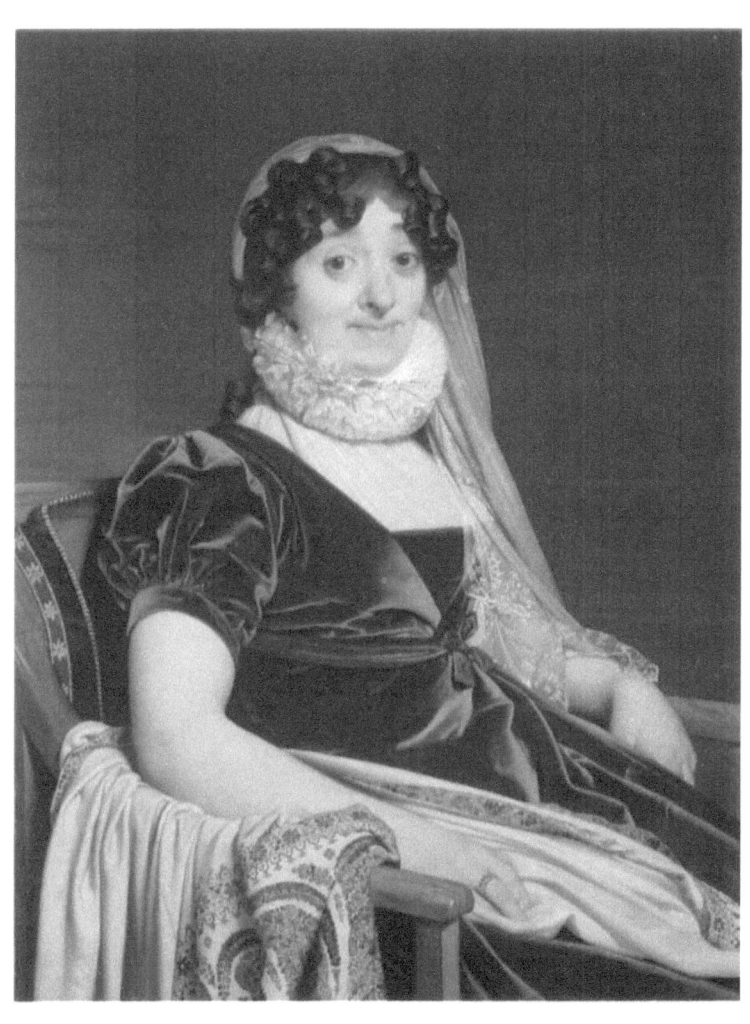

Comtes de Tournon, née Geneviève de Seytres
Caumont, 1812, oil on canvas

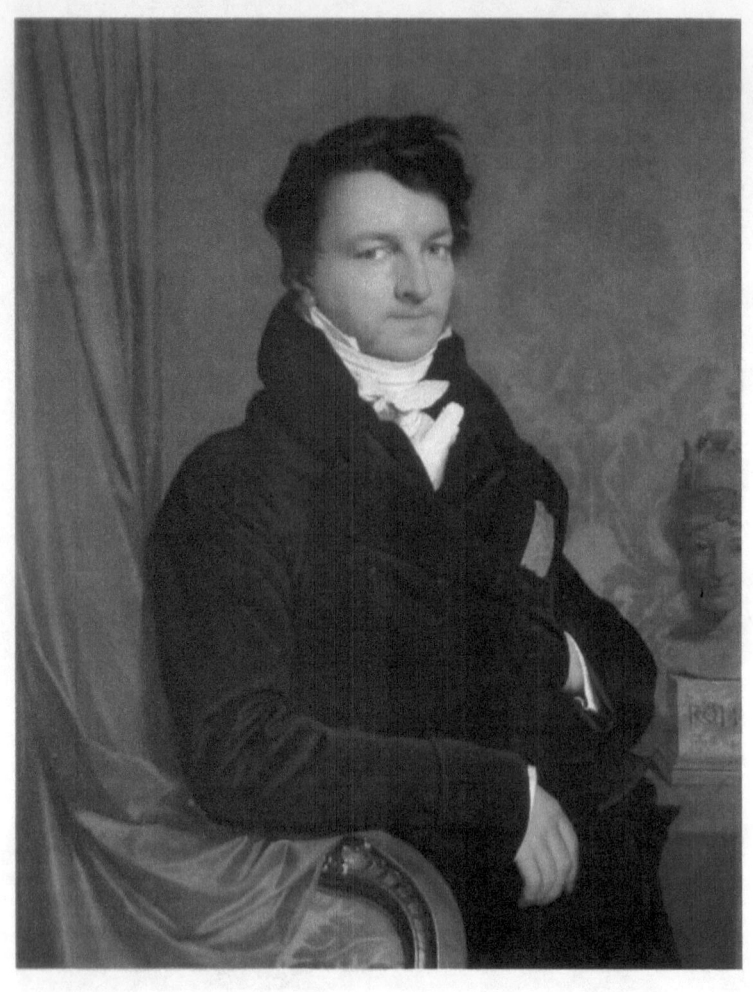

Monsieur de Norvins, 1811-1812, oil on canvas

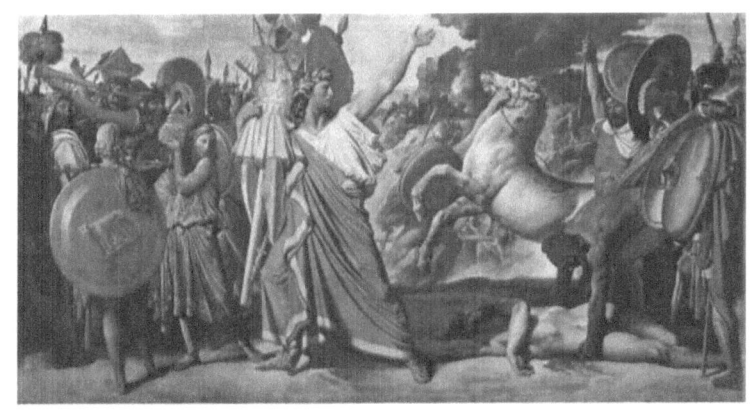

Romulus' Victory over Acron, 1812, oil on canvas

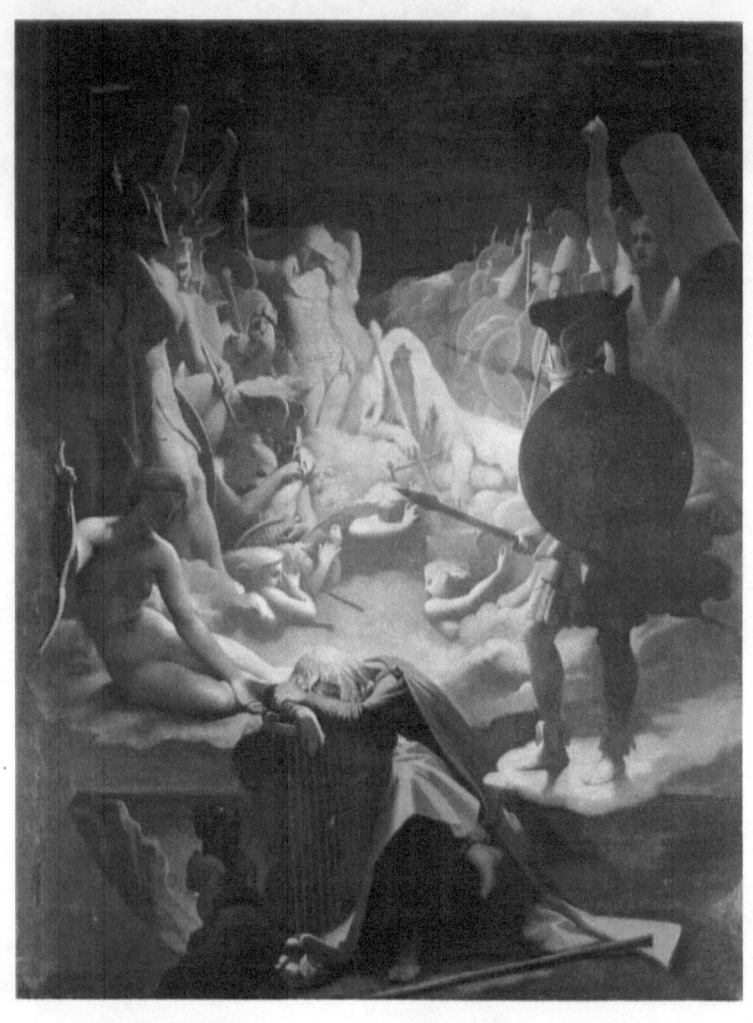

The Dream of Ossian, 1813, oil on canvas

Ossian purports to be a translation of an epic cycle of Scottish poems from the early dark ages. Ossian, a blind bard, sings of the life and battles of Fingal, a Scotch warrior. Ossian caused a sensation when it was published on the cusp of the era of revolutions, and had a massive cultural impact during the 18th and 19th centuries. Napoleon carried a copy into battle; Goethe translated parts of it; the city of Selma, Alabama was named after the home of Fingal, and one of Ingres' most romantic and moody paintings, the Dream of Ossian was based on it. The originator of the "unearthed, old Irish fragments" Fingal and Temora, published in 1762 and 1763, was a Scot, James Macpherson (1736-1796). Ten years after Macpherson's death it was discovered that the poems were forgeries, written by Macpherson himself from fragments of sagas.

In 1812 Ingres was commissioned to paint the subject of Ossian for the ceiling of one of the rooms used by Napoleon in the Quirinal Palace in Rome. Three years after Napoleon left, the Pope gave the painting back to the artist, understandably, for the heathen visions were hardly suitable for the Catholic ambience.

Ingres handled the theme with monumental simplicity. The dream figures are like transparent alabaster sculptures, they look exhausted, lying almost lifeless, as if they themselves are dreaming the dream. The work has a timeless, dreamlike quality.

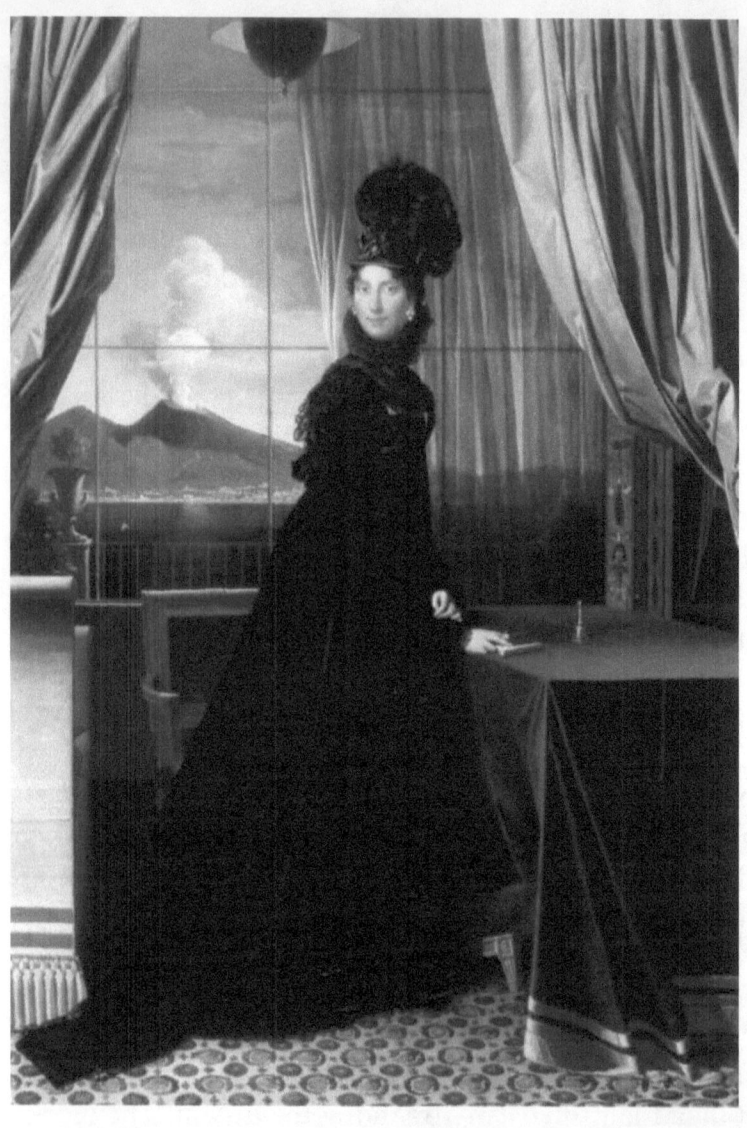

Caroline Murat, Queen of Naples, 1814, oil on canvas

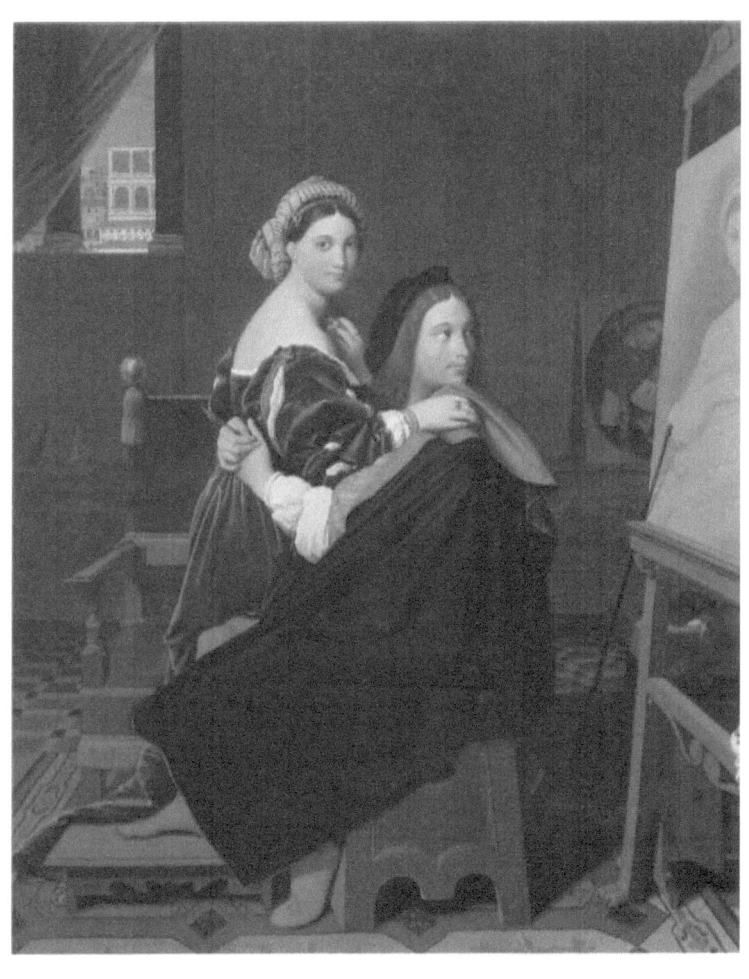

Raphael and the Fornarina, 1814, oil on canvas

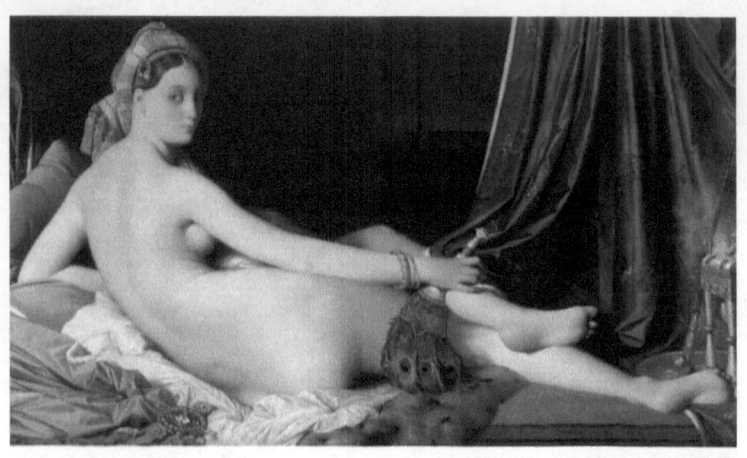

The Grande Odalisque, 1814, oil on canvas

The effects in Ingres' paintings largely depend on drawing and linearity, but he also used colour to supremely calculated effect. The cold turquoise of the silk curtain with its decoration of red flowers intensified the warm flesh tone of the Grande Odalisque. This nude was painted in 1814 for Napoleon's sister, Queen Caroline Murat. Unlike the realism of Goya's Maja, Ingres' nude is hardly intimate, the eroticism here emerging slowly from the reserve and the questioning, assessing glance of the naked woman. This is a tradition that goes back to Giorgione and Titian, but Ingres has painted a living woman and not an allegory of Venus. Nevertheless, the realistic intimacy is lessened by setting the scene in the distant world of the Orient.

For many in the West, the idea of the harem with its available or exploited women trapped in their own closed world was as much proof of the fallen or primitive state of the East as was its supposed savagery. But it was also infinitely titillating. Ingres's picture is more than this, however. A sense of loss was inevitably embodied in French perceptions of the East after their defeat in Egypt, and it was perhaps because it sublimated unattainable desires that the theme of the Oriental nude, bather or harem girl gained such a haunting appeal. Ingres is remarkable for combining a frank allure with a chilling perfection of flesh. He had picked up his discreet hints of the harem — a turban here, a fan there — from Oriental artefacts and miniatures in the collections of Gros and Denon. They serve to locate his nude, who otherwise could really belong anywhere, in a sensuous Orient of the imagination.

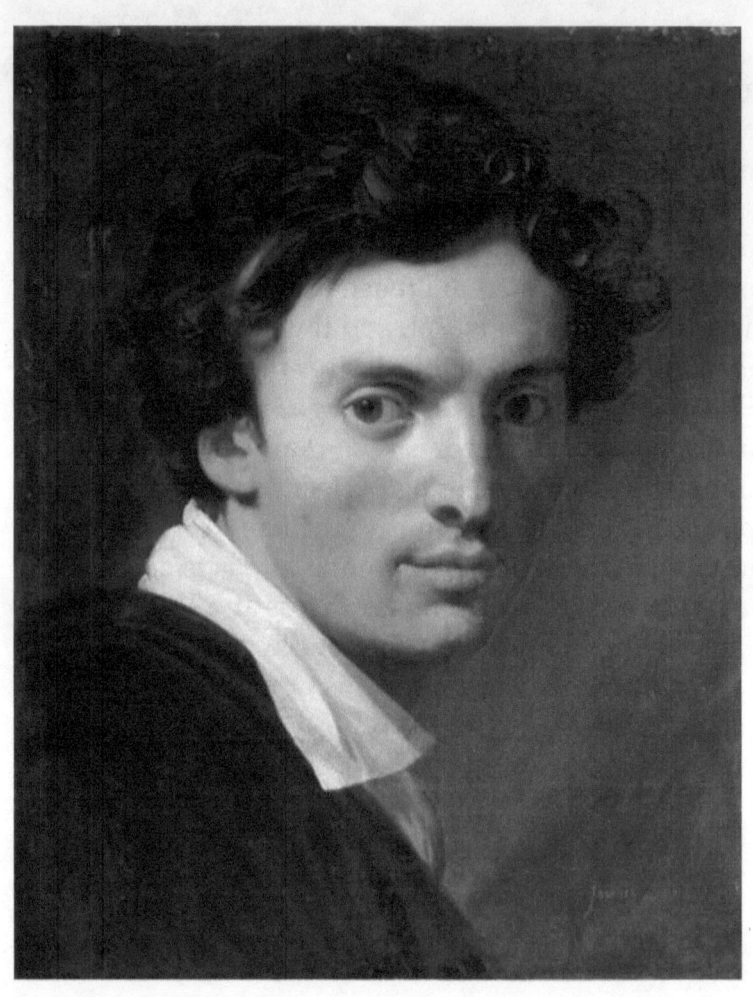

Jean Pierre Cortot, 1815, oil on canvas

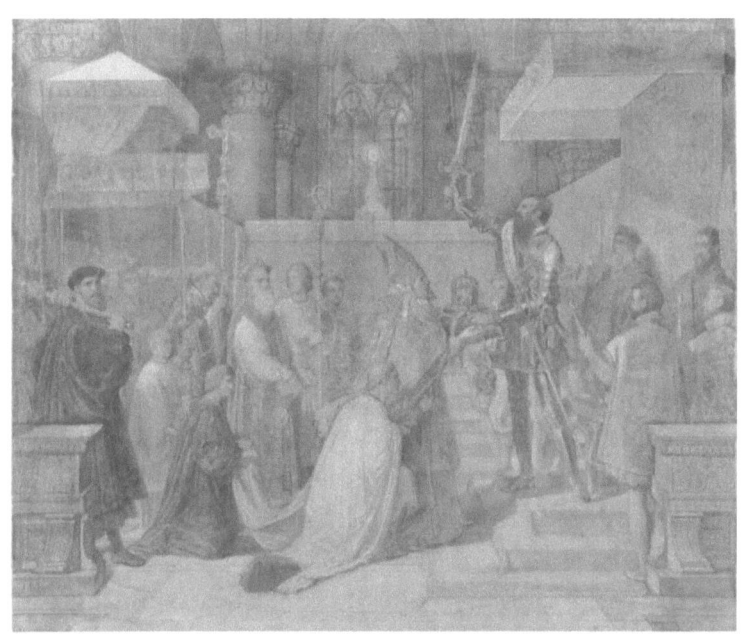

The Duke of Alba Receiving the Pope's Blessing in the Cathedral of St.-Gudule, Brussels, 1815, Pen and brown ink, and brown wash, heightened with white, with graphite, black and red chalk

Jean-Auguste-Dominique Ingres made this drawing either as a preparatory sketch or as a presentation drawing for a commission that he accepted in 1815 because he was financially strapped. The fourteenth Duke of Alba ordered a painting to commemorate the third Duke of Alba, also known as the "Butcher of Flanders." Here the infamous ancestor receives a hat and sword blessed by the pope for suppressing Protestant heresy in the Netherlands. As the governor-general of the Netherlands from 1567 to 1573, the duke had formed the Council of Troubles, nicknamed the "Council of Blood," which condemned some 12,000 Protestant rebels to death.

The drawing took many hours to make, including constructing a complicated cut-out replacement to correct the architectural background. Despite reworking the picture into a red-dominated composition symbolizing a bloodbath, Ingres, repulsed, abandoned the painting in 1819. He later said that the painting remained a sketch-"as God had wished." Edgar Degas, a great admirer of Ingres, once owned the unfinished canvas. During World War II, Hermann Goering acquired the painting; at war's end it went to the Musée Ingres at Montauban, France.

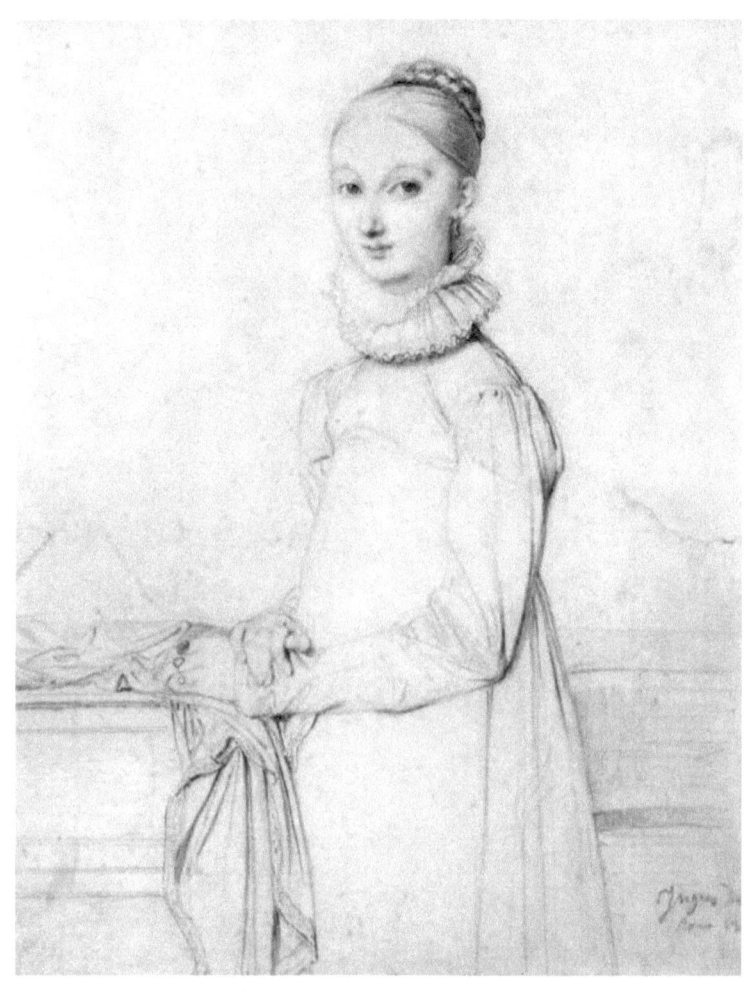

Portrait of a Girl, c. 1815, Graphite pencil on paper, 280
x 207 mm
Affection for this model (probably a relative of Lucien
Bonaparte, Napoleon's brother) imbues the artist's line
with a natural suppleness and precision. Without
striving after psychological insight, Ingres brings out
the mix of stiffness and femininity behind his subject's
cool gaze.

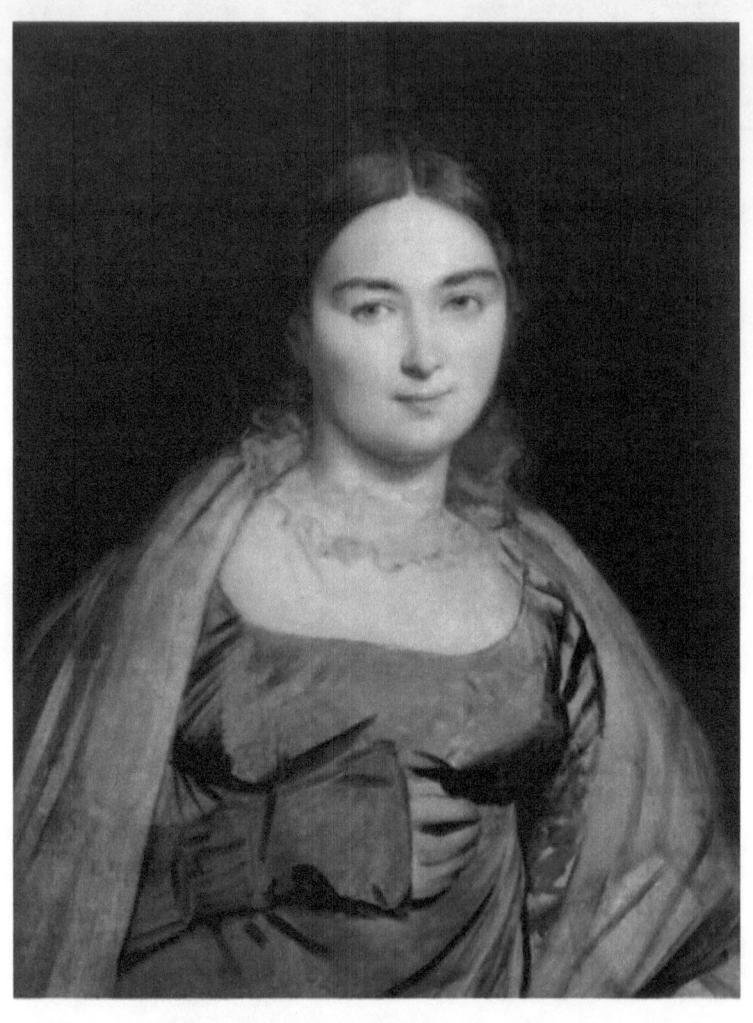

Portrait of Madame Ingres, 1815, oil on canvas

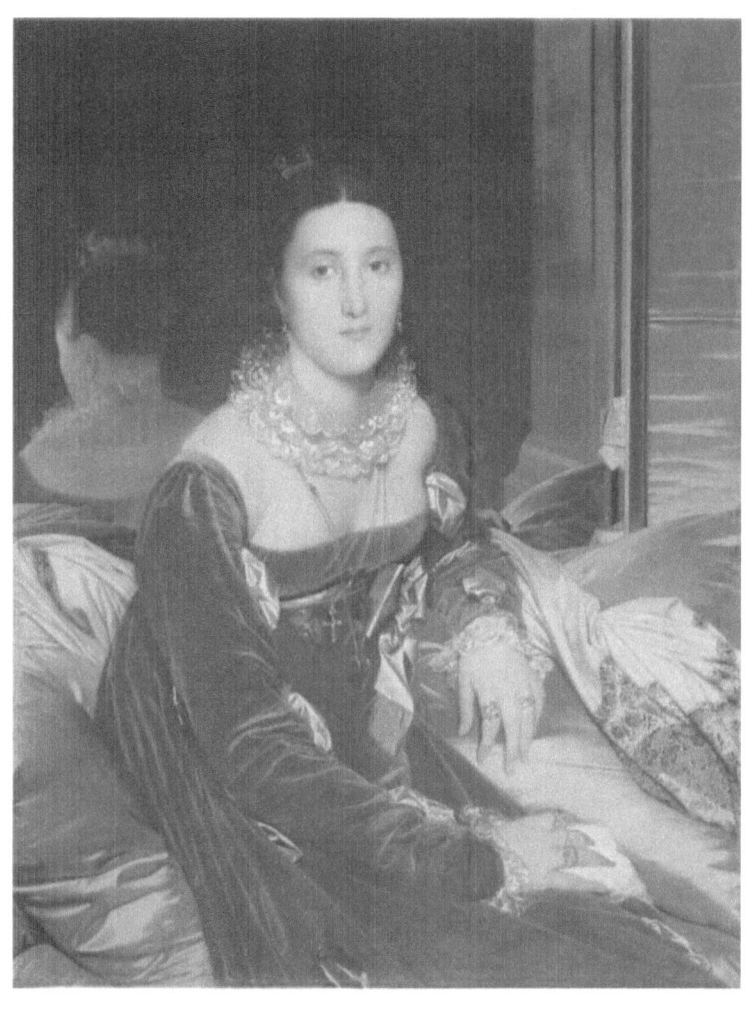

Portrait of Madame de Senonnes, c.1814-c.1816, oil on canvas

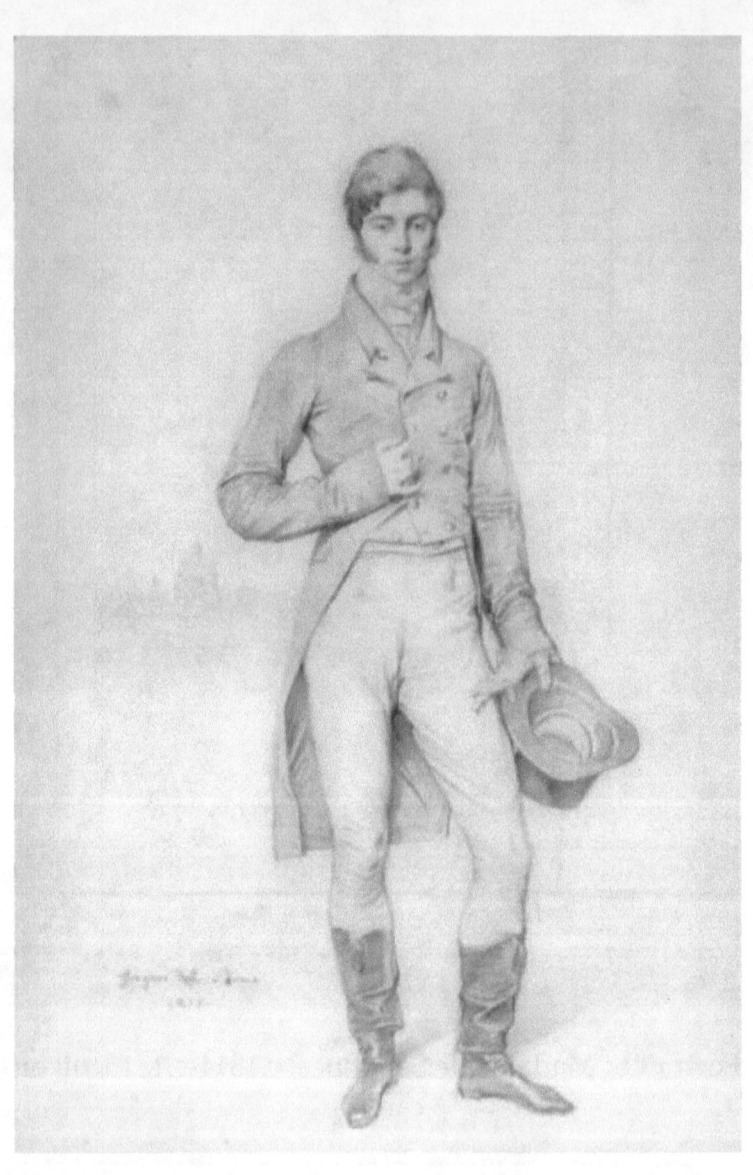

Portrait of Lord Grantham, 1816, Graphite

Thomas Robinson, the third Baron Grantham and later Earl de Grey, was thirty-five when Jean-Auguste-Dominique Ingres drew this refined portrait. Ingres chose a pose that combined the informality of youth and the self-assurance of his subject's aristocratic origins. Grantham, who commissioned this portrait himself, stands confidently against a distant view of Saint Peter's Basilica, an important site for Grand Tourists and one that Ingres often included in portraits. Ingres made this drawing when he was a struggling young artist living in Rome, earning his living by drawing portraits of wealthy visitors to the city.

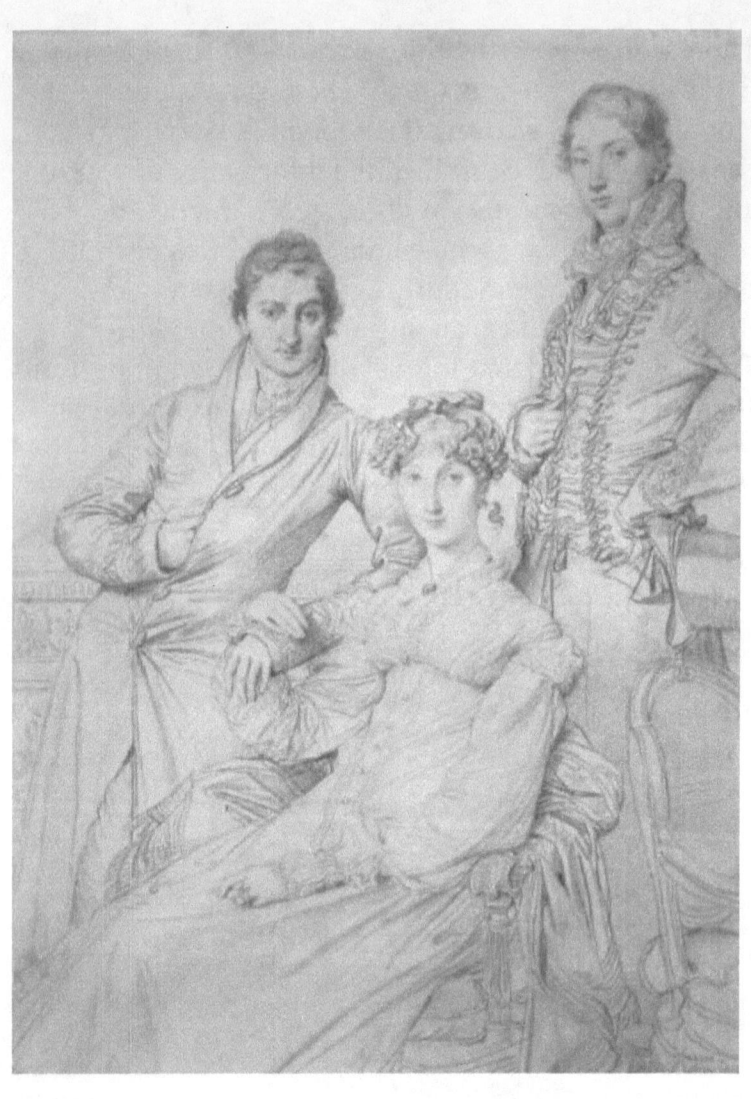

Mr and Mrs Joseph Woodhead and Mr Henry Comber
in Rome, 1816, Graphite

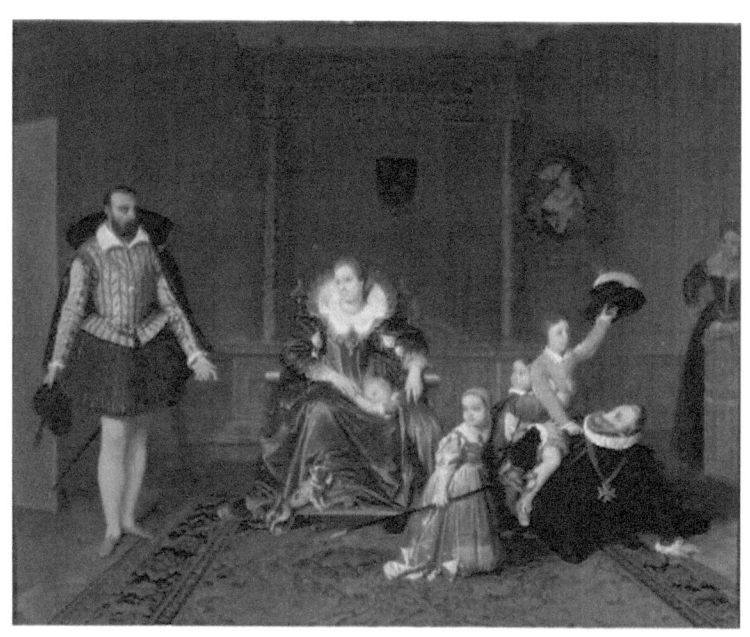

Henry IV Recieving The Ambassador of Spain, 1817, oil on canvas

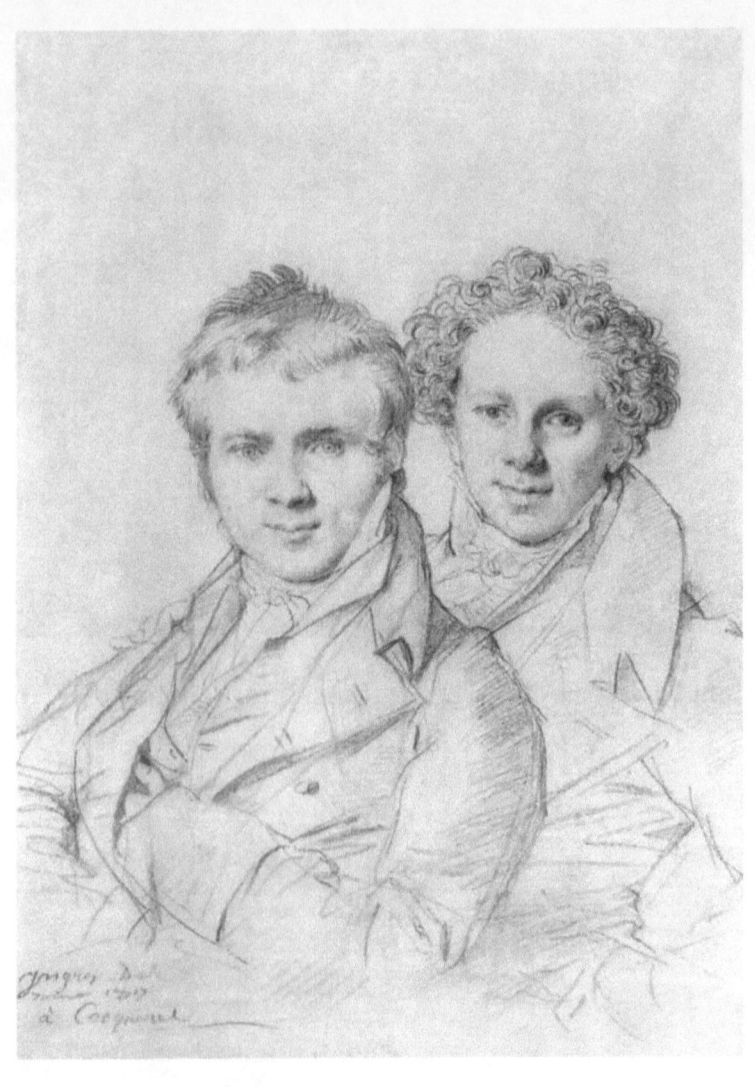

Double Portrait of Otto Magnus von Stackelberg and
Jacob Linckh, 1817, Graphite, 194 x 144 mm

The tiny drawing represents Count Otto Magnus Baron von Stackelberg, one of the first archaeologists, and also a writer, painter and art historian, born in Tallinn (on the right), and probably Jakob Linckh, a German painter and archaeologist. Both young men were at the age of 31 at the time Ingres had sketched them.

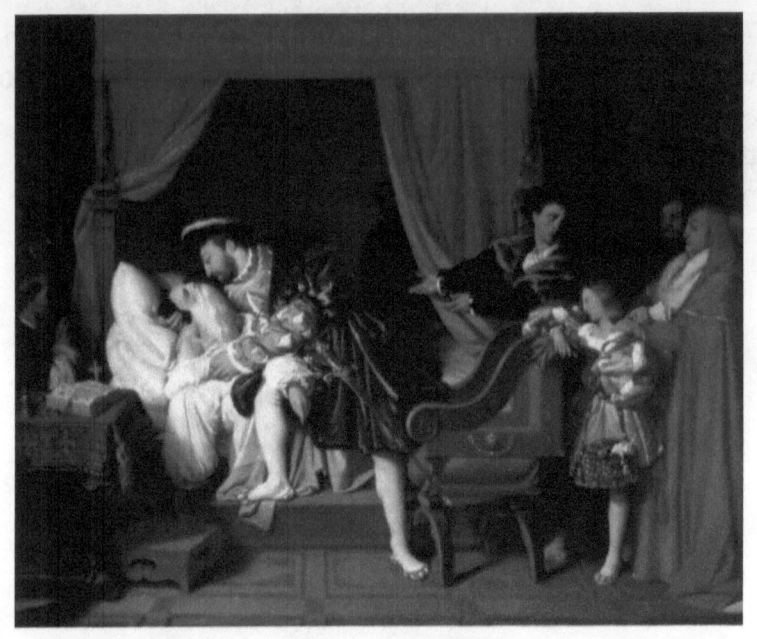

Death of Leonardo da Vinci, 1818, oil on canvas

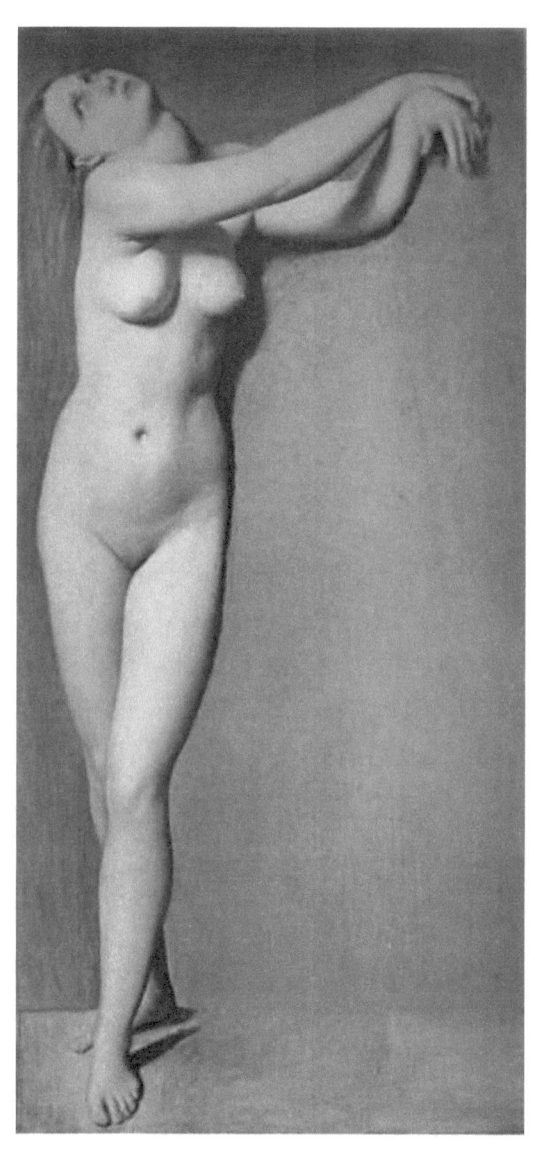

Angelica, Study for the Roger Delivering Angelica,
1819, oil on canvas

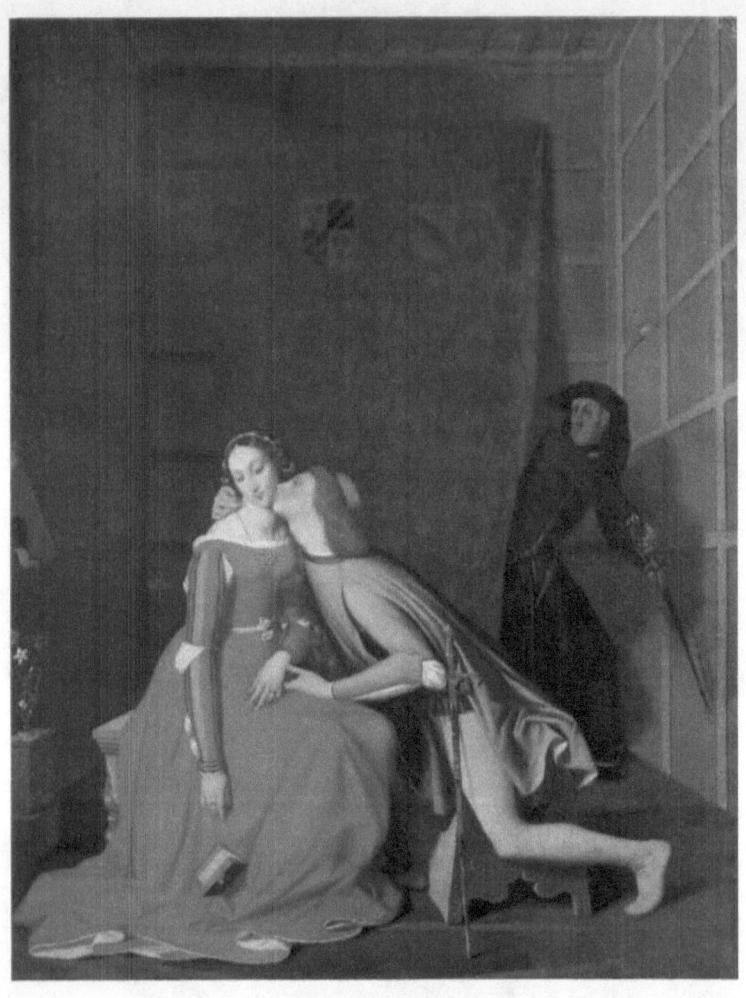

Francesca da Rimini and Paolo Malatesta, 1819, oil on
canvas
The influence of German artists on Ingres should be
mentioned. While in Italy he became familiar with the
paintings of German painters (Julius Schnorr von
Carolsfeld, Friedrich Overbeck, Peter Cornelius and
others). Many of Ingres' paintings reflect these
encounters such as the Paolo and Francesca.

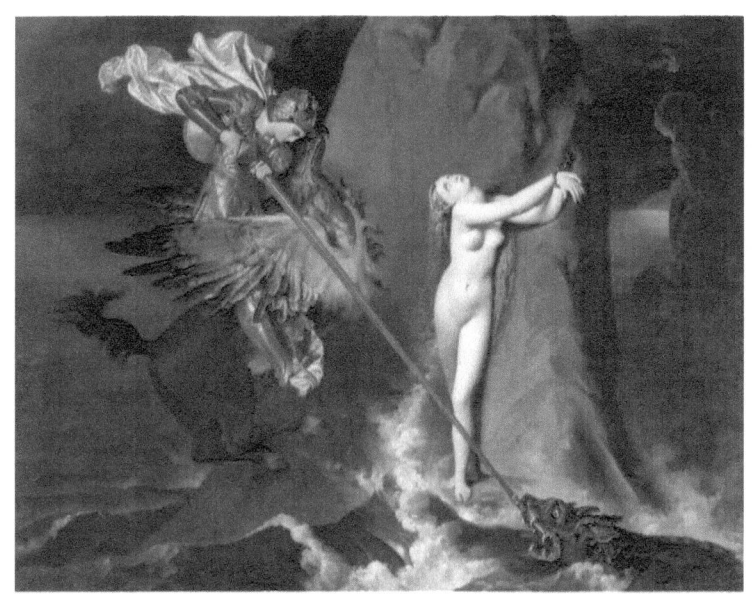

Roger Delivering Angelica, 1819, oil on canvas

Angelica is the daughter of a king of Cathay in Orlando Furioso, by the Italian poet Ariosto (1474-1533), a romantic epic poem about the conflict between Christians and Saracens at the time of Charlemagne. Angelica was loved by several knights, Christian and pagan, among them the Christian hero Orlando (Roland). He was maddened (furioso) with grief and jealousy because she became the lover of, and eventually married, the Moor Modero. Roger (Ruggiero) freeing Angelica is a theme very like Perseus and Andromeda. Angelica chained to a rock by the seashore is about to be attacked by a sea-monster, the orc. Roger, one of the pagan champions, arrives riding on a hippogriff (a monster, the creation of the poets of the late middle ages). He dazzles the monster with his magic shield, and places a magic ring on Angelica's finger to protect her. He undoes her bonds and they ride off together.

Ingres developed a highly sensitive aestheticism, particularly in depicting the beautiful naked body. He excelled his teachers in this, and it was here that he sought an ideal of form that goes to the limits of what can be done in painting. It is hard to find an equal anywhere in the history of art turned to us by The Grand Odalisque or the body of the young girl in Roger Freeing Angelica, modeled in soft lines.

The position of the young Angelica, with her head tilted back, is highly exaggerated by modern standards, but the exposed and defenseless neck and the eyes cast up to suggest that she has fainted are intended to signalise pure feminine submission. In order to portray this unconditional surrender to her rescuer, Ingres has almost made her look as if she has goitre. But this calculated submission to the aesthetic of the nude makes it no less erotic precisely because the very evidence of a weak spot in her beauty makes her seem less remote from the viewer.

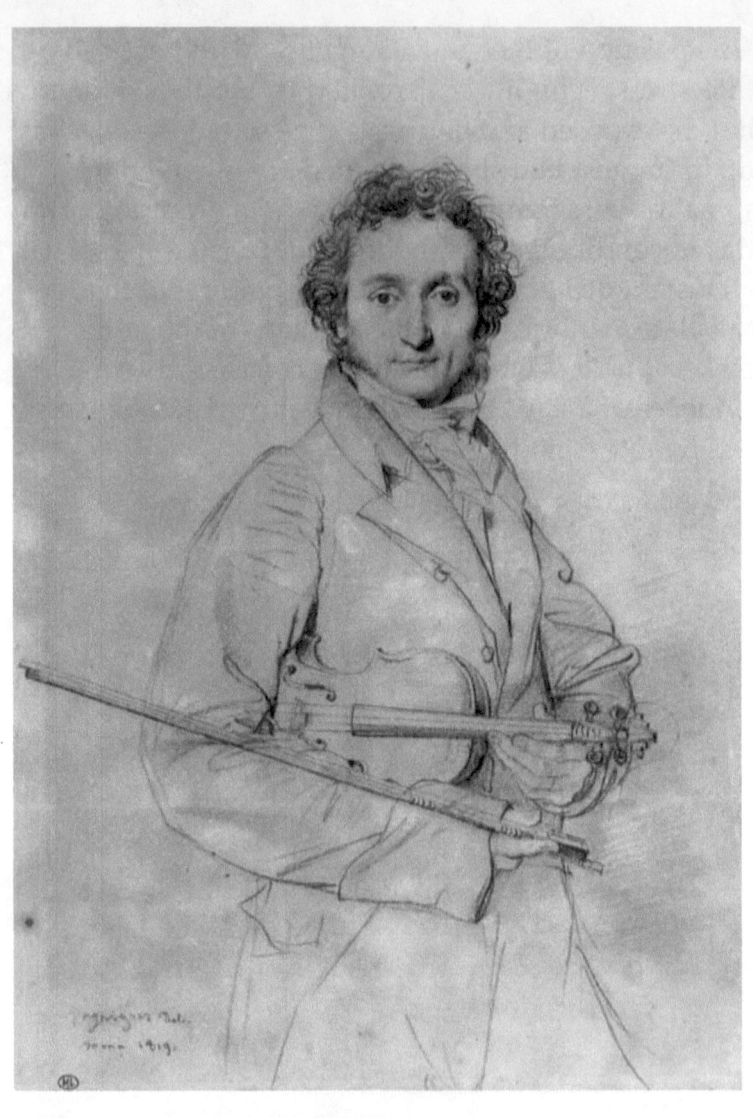

The Violinist Niccolò Paganini, 1819, Pencil, 298 x 218 mm

Ingres was a life-long proponent of the primacy of line over colour. His service to art lay in his abilities as a portraitist and as one of the most important draughtsmen of the century. His portrait drawings are remarkable for their psychological empathy and the enormous subtlety with which light and surface area are treated. Ingres, himself a talented violinist, drew a portrait of Niccolò Paganini - at that stage at the very beginning of his career - probably as a reminder of concerts the two friends had performed together.

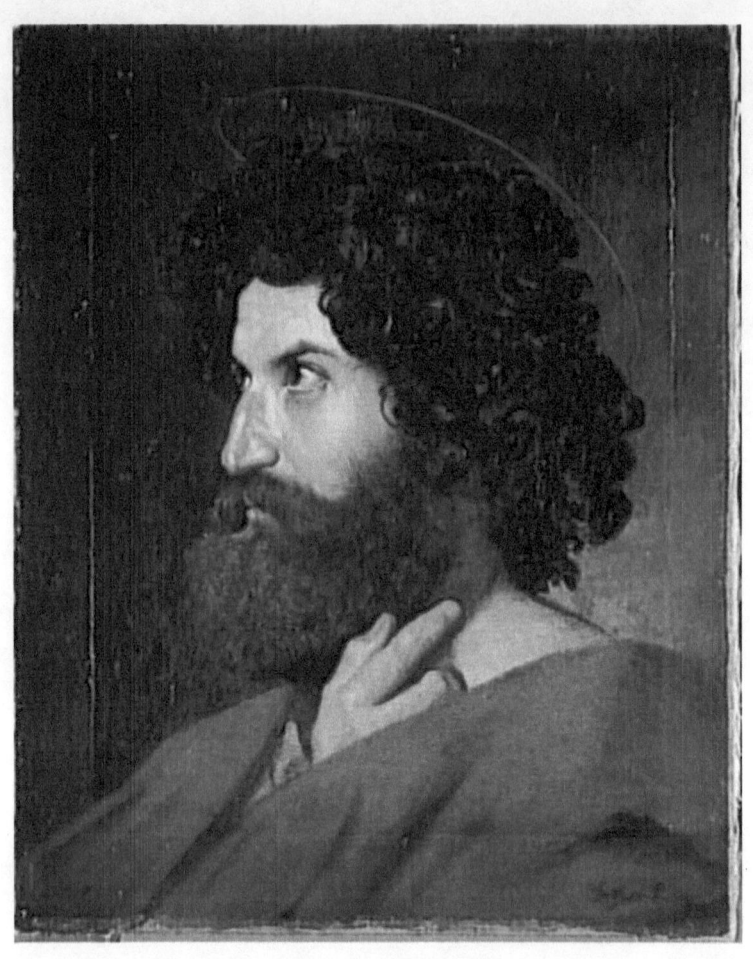

Head of St. Matthew, 1820, oil on canvas

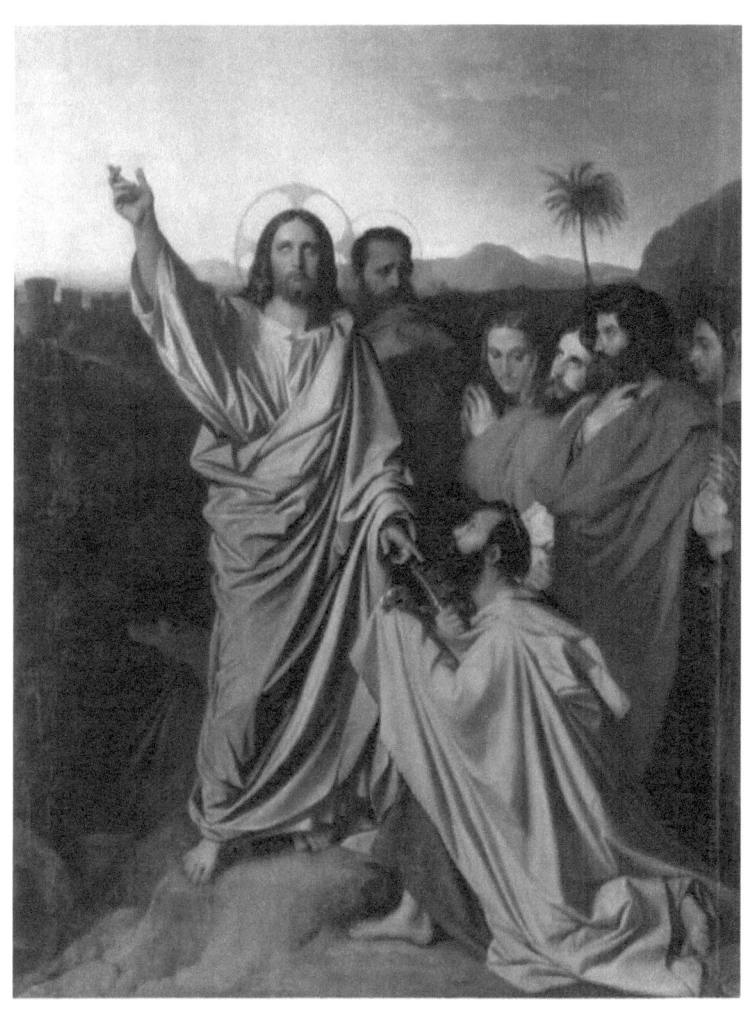

Jesus Returning the Keys to St. Peter, 1820, oil on canvas

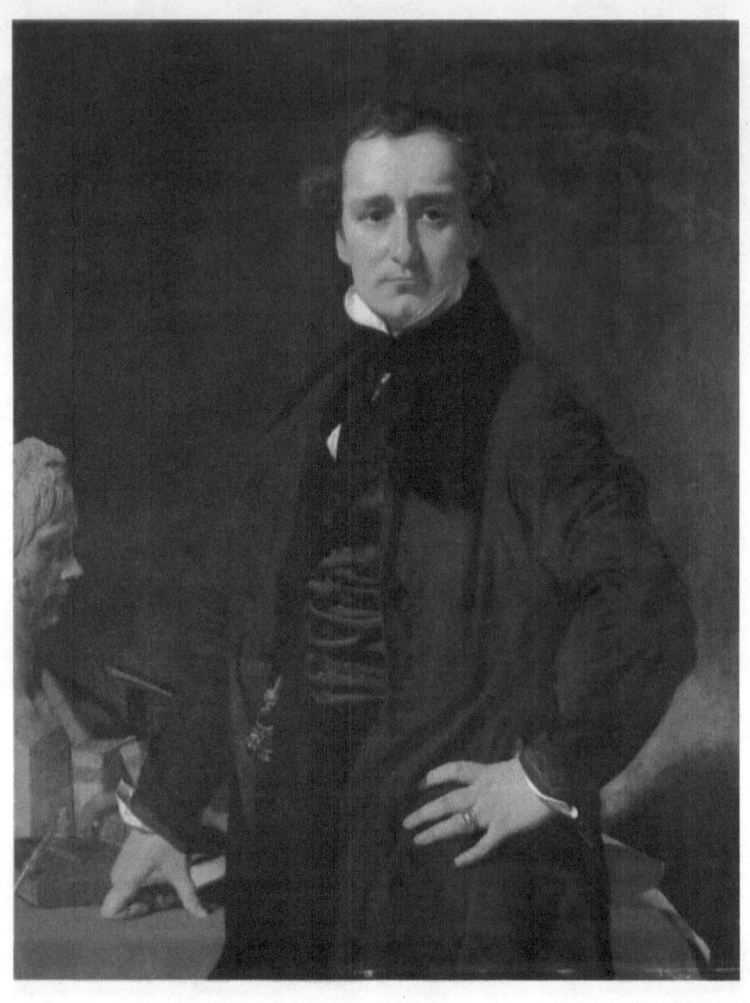

Portrait of the Sculptor Lorenzo Bartolini, 1820, oil on
canvas

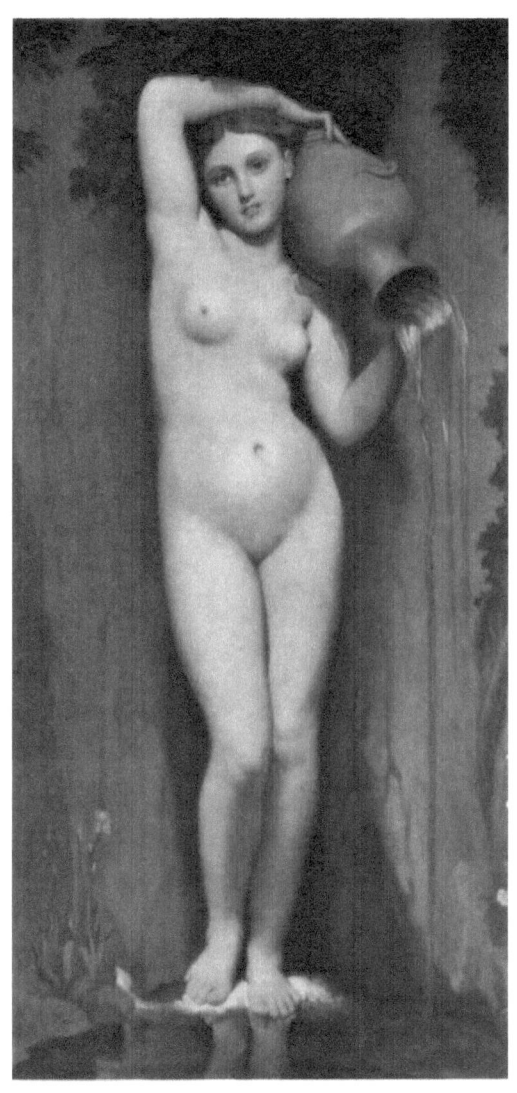

The Source, 1820, Oil on canvas, 83 x 163 cm
Ingres began this painting in Florence in 1820 but
finished it much later in Paris with the assistants
Alexandre Legoffe and Jean Paul Etienne Balze.

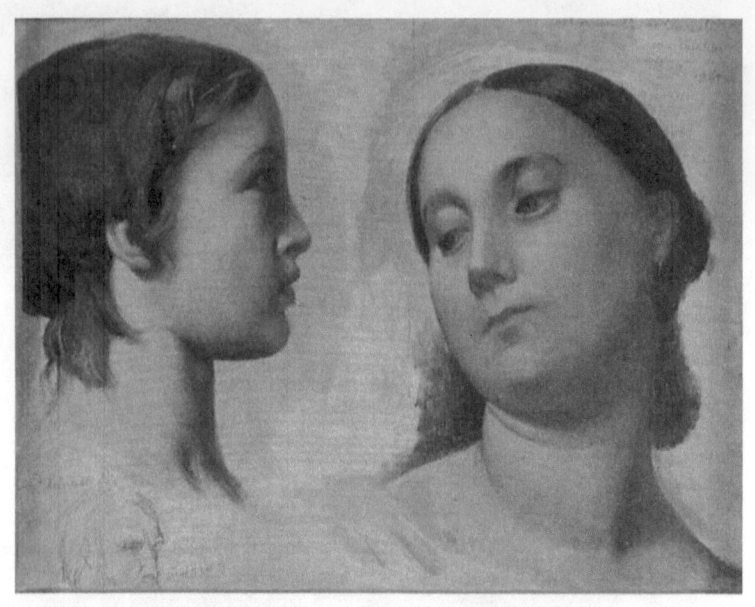

Madame and her son Lauréal, 1821, oil on canvas

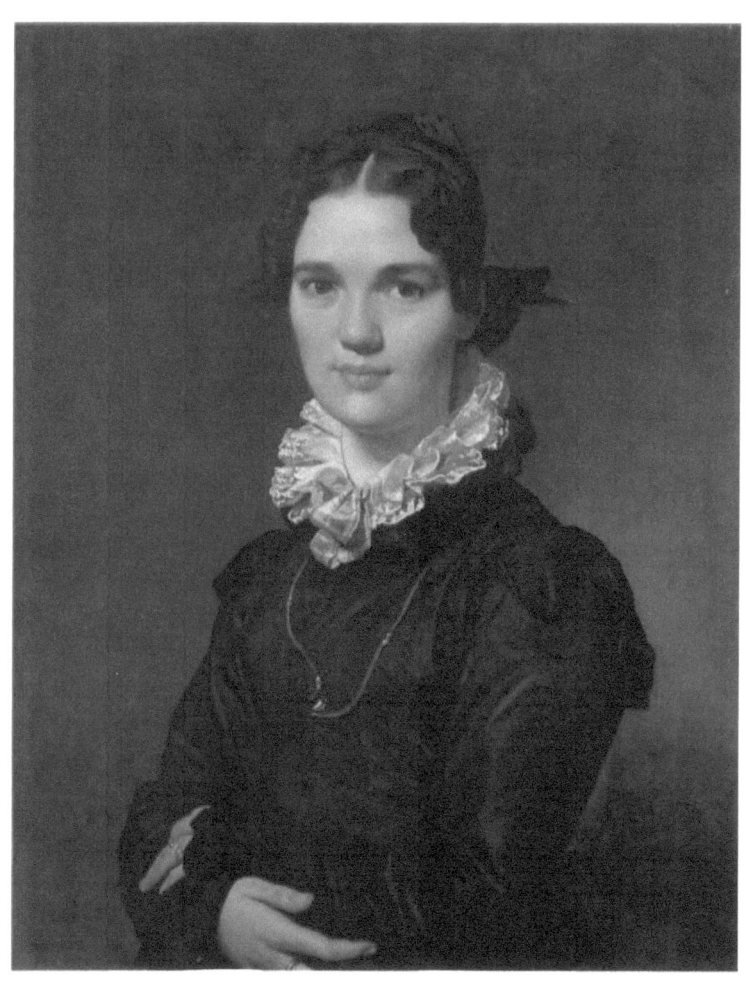

Mademoiselle Jeanne Gonin, 1821, oil on canvas

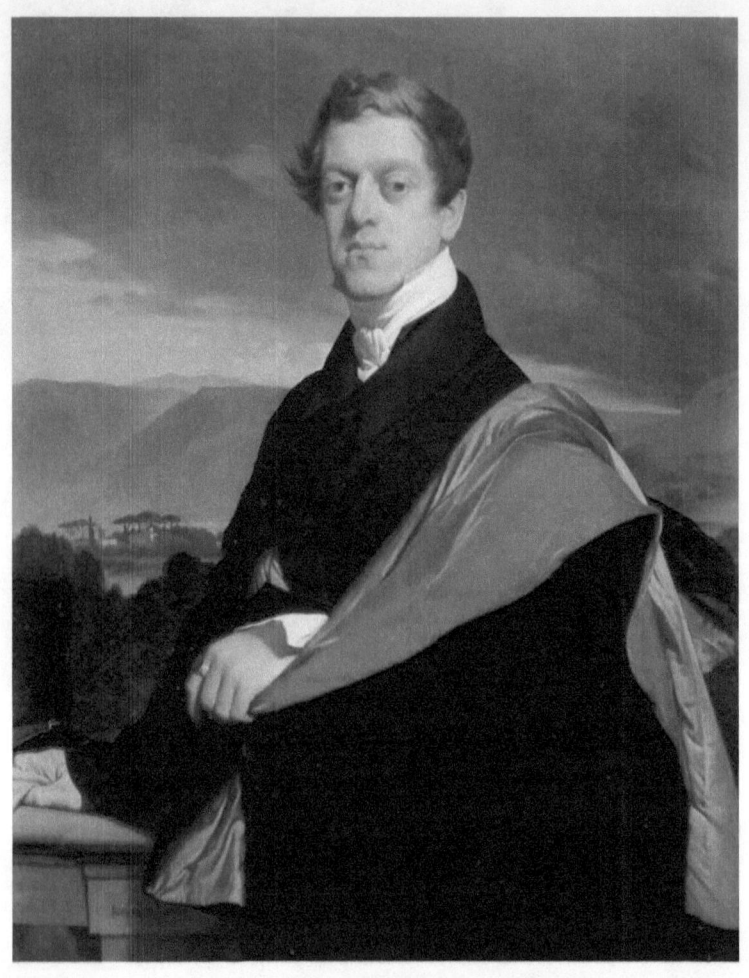

Portrait of Count Nikolay Gouriev, 1821, oil on canvas
In this portrait of a Russian diplomat, Ingres does not idealize his subject but uses him as a pretext for the expression of his own conception of the ideal. Despite being a cold combination of classical clichŭs, the work remains a model of perfection in line and composition. Such a dramatic colour range is rare for Ingres and is reminiscent of portraits by Florentine Mannerists, one of the greatest impressions the artist gained from Italy.

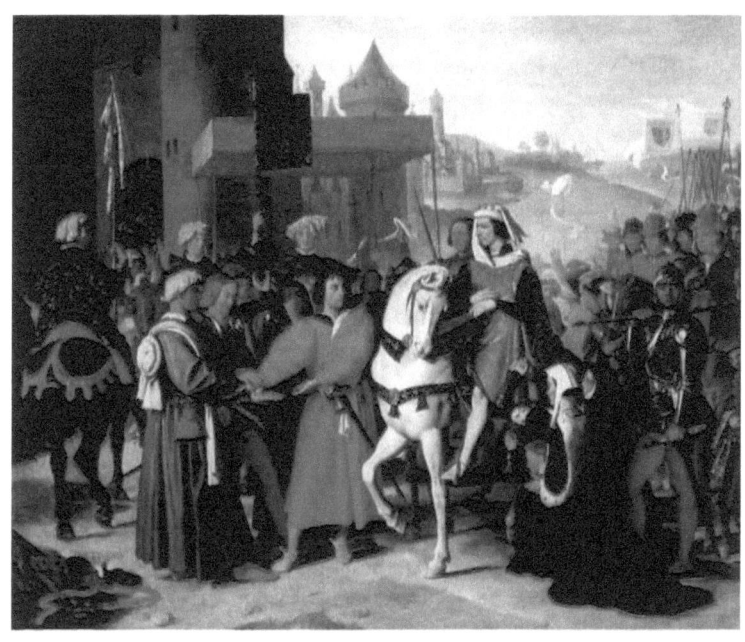

The Entry of the Future Charles V into Paris in 1358, 1821, Oil on canvas, 47 x 56 cm

The influence of German artists on Ingres should be mentioned. While in Italy he became familiar with the paintings of German painters (Julius Schnorr von Carolsfeld, Friedrich Overbeck, Peter Cornelius and others). Many of Ingres' paintings reflect these encounters, particularly The Entry of the Future Charles V into Paris in 1358.

This piece of blatant Bourbon propaganda was created for the pro-Bourbon comte Amedñe-David de Pastoret - of whom Ingres was to paint a splendid portrait for the Salon of 1827 - and shows his ancestor, Jean Pastourel, a fourteenth-century president of the Paris parliament, greeting the future king at the city gates after he had survived a peasants' insurrection in 1358. The subject, taken from the fourteenth-century chronicles of Jean Froissart, was matched in an appropriately archaic style.

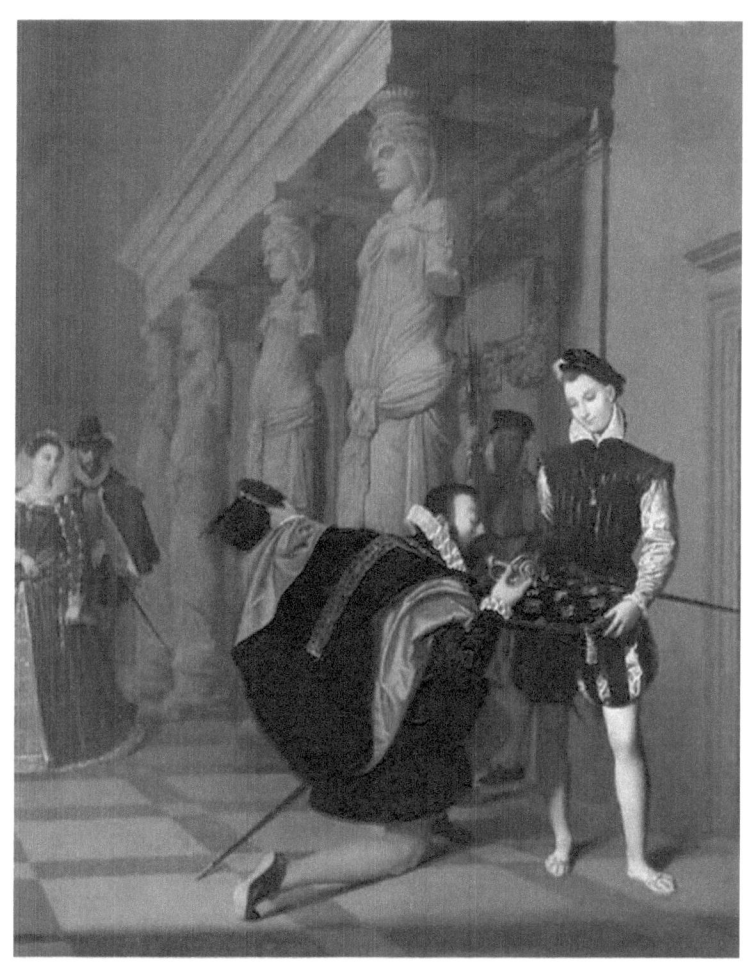

Don Pedro of Toledo Kissing the Sword of Henri IV,
1822, Oil on panel, 49 x 41 cm

Of the known versions of Don Pedro of Toledo Kissing
the Sword of Henri IV, the present picture is the most
striking, due primarily to the dramatic perspective of
the Salle des Caryatides. Although this painting was
signed and dated Rome 1820, Ingres had originally
entered it in the 1814 Salon, but then reworked it,
finally completing the painting in 1822.

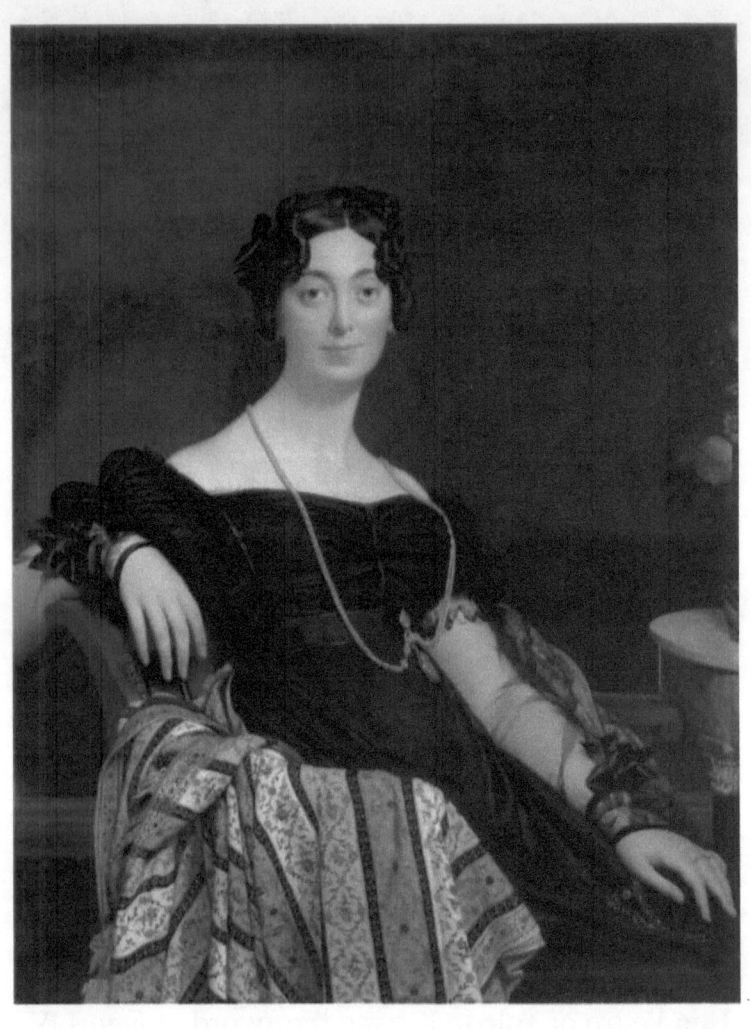

Portrait of Madame Leblanc, 1823, oil on canvas

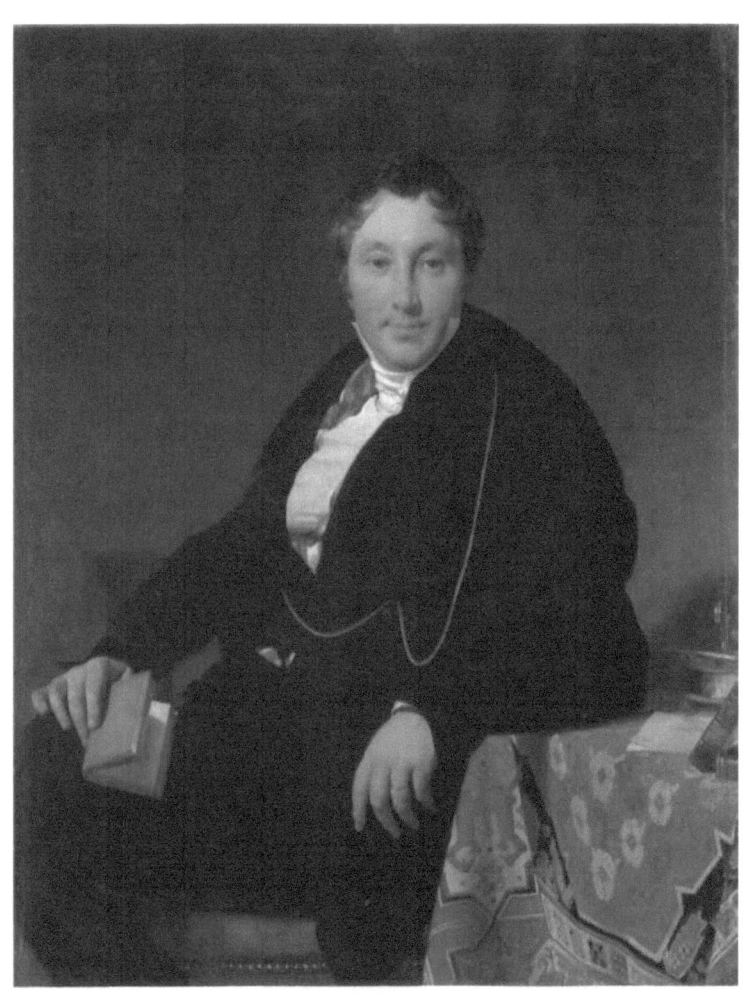

Portrait of Monsieur Leblanc, c.1823, oil on canvas

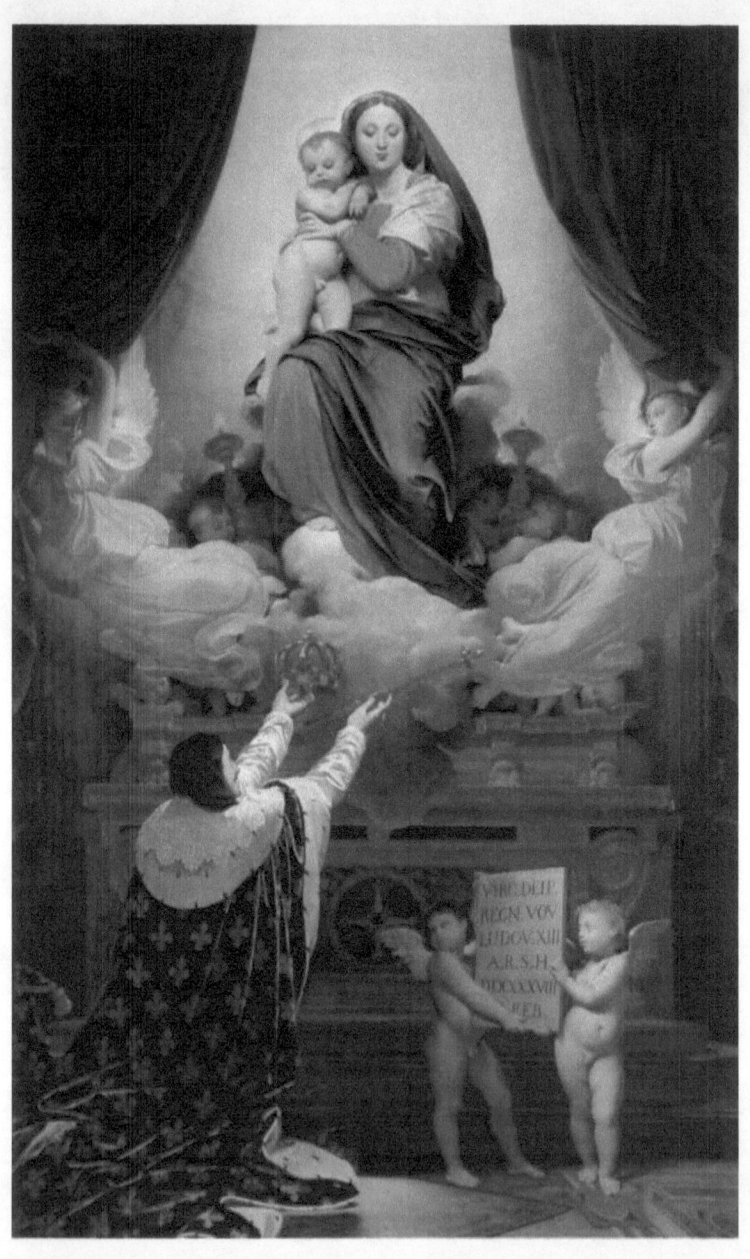

The Vow of Louis XIII, 1824, oil on canvas

Ingres continued to paint in the Neoclassical style throughout his career, although the style came under attack from younger contemporaries like Gũricault or Delacroix. The Vow of Louis XIII is a kind of neoclassical votive painting. In it Ingres adapted whole passages of Raphael's Madonna di Foligno, but he also borrowed forms that were developed by the Carraccis.

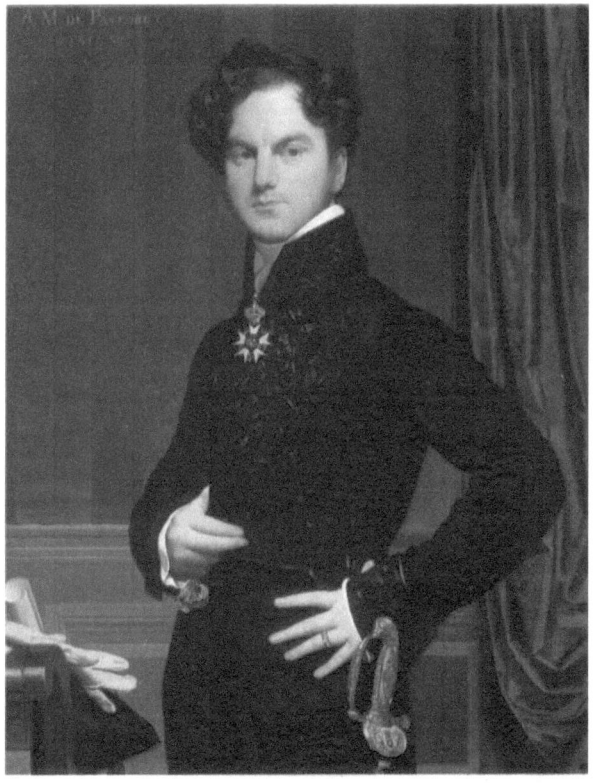

Amedee-David, the Comte de Pastoret, 1823-1826, oil on canvas

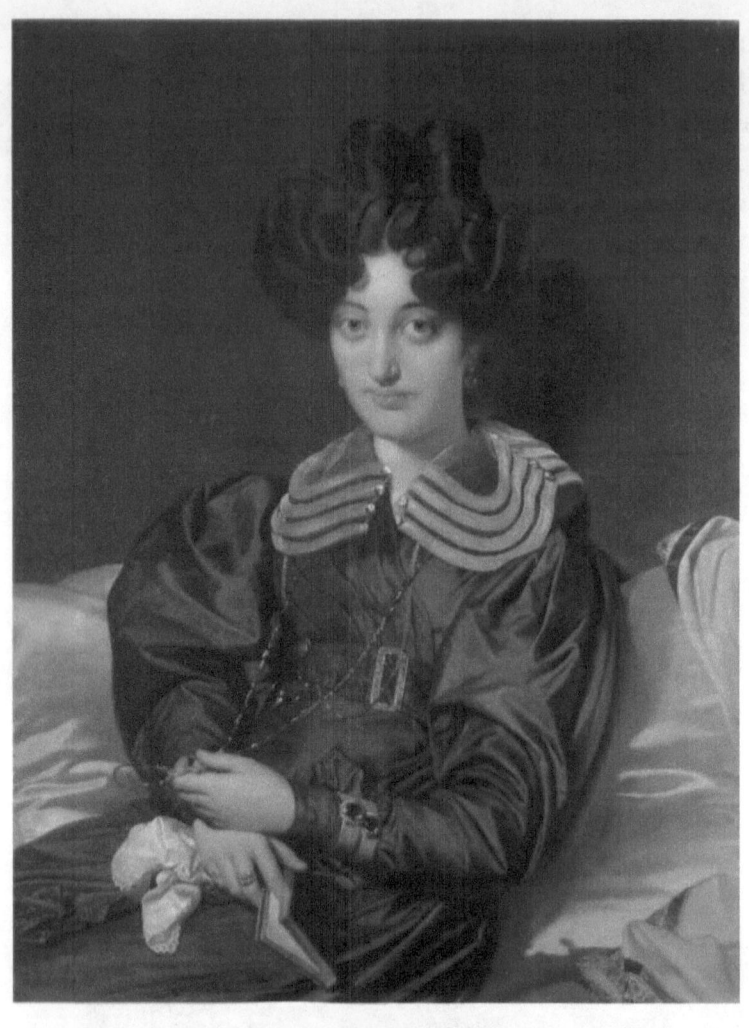

Portrait of Madame Marcotte de Sainte-Marie, 1826, oil on canvas

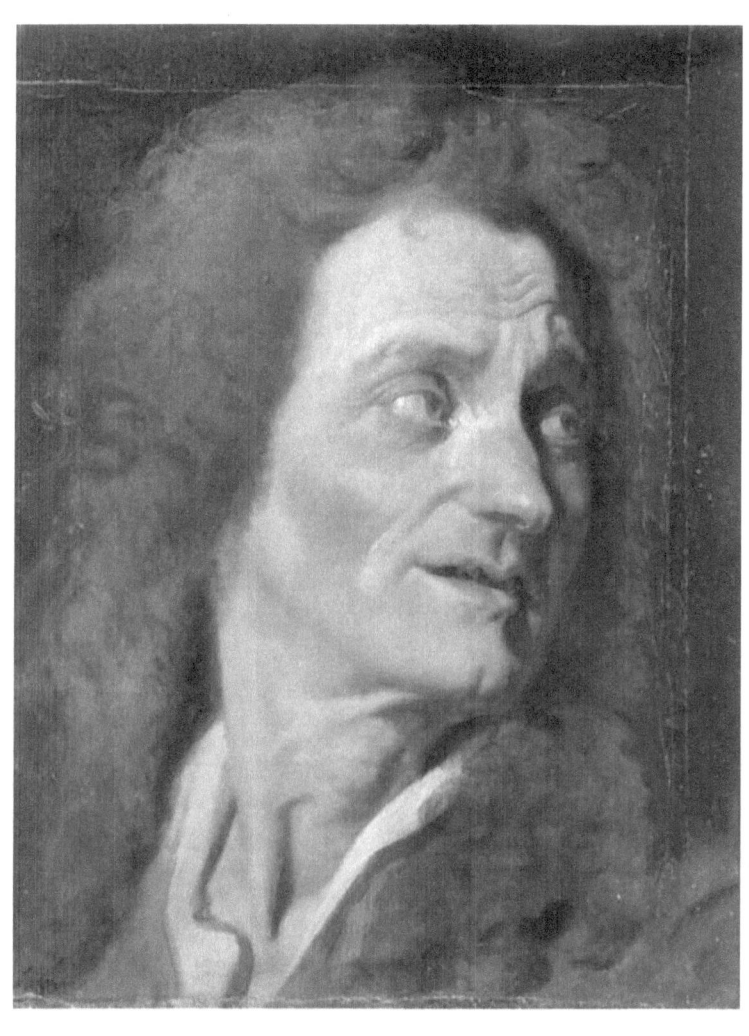

Head of Boileau, 1827, oil on canvas

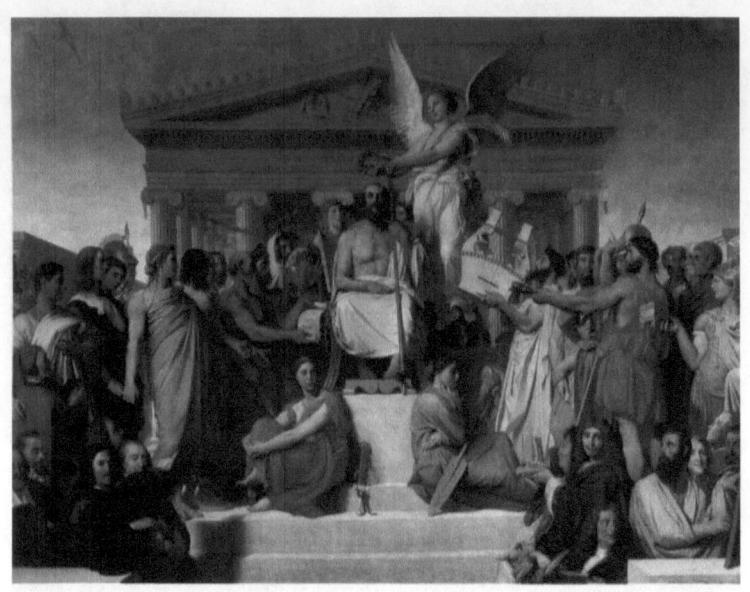

The Apotheosis of Homer, 1827, Oil on canvas, 386 x 512 cm

Ingres attempted in 1827 a historical synopsis in his great composition, the Apotheosis of Homer. This canvas was originally a ceiling decoration in the Salle Clarac in the Louvre.

The most famous artists in history are depicted here: Dante and Moliиre and painters such as Poussin, but Homer reigns above them all. This assembly of great artists and writers of all ages gathered to honour the ancient Greek poet before a classical temple might look the epitome of hierarchical academicism. The painting was intended as the sum of all aesthetic rules. However, it could hardly live up to the expectations. Today it seems stiff and unnatural.

The painting's formal composition and pale, sugary colours appear at the opposite extreme to Delacroix's Sardanapalus, shown in the same Salon. Delacroix's picture seems far away from academic orthodoxy, while Ingres's Homer looks like its ultimate endorsement.

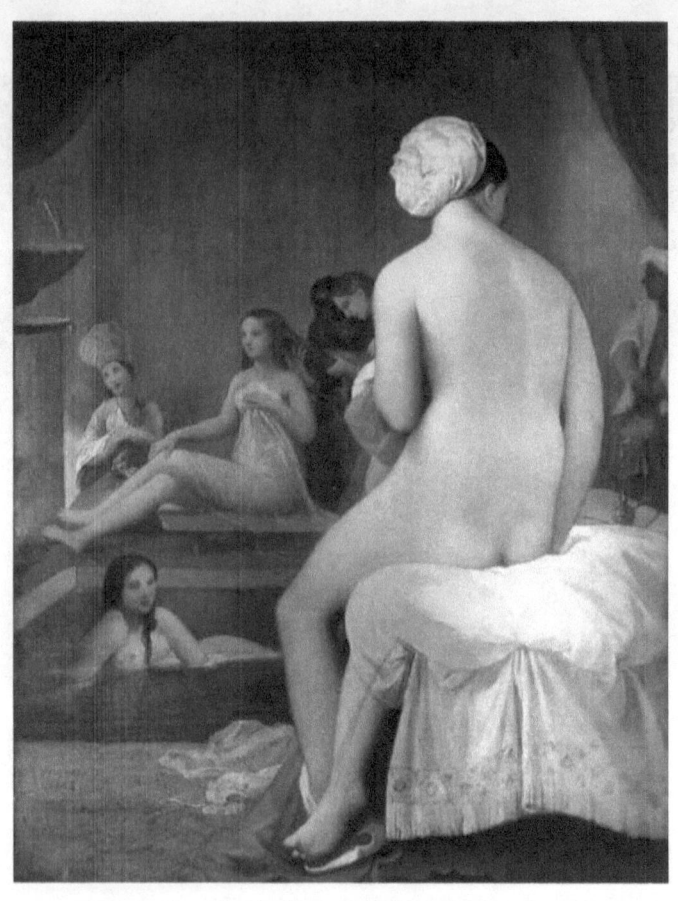

The Small Bather, 1828, oil on canvas

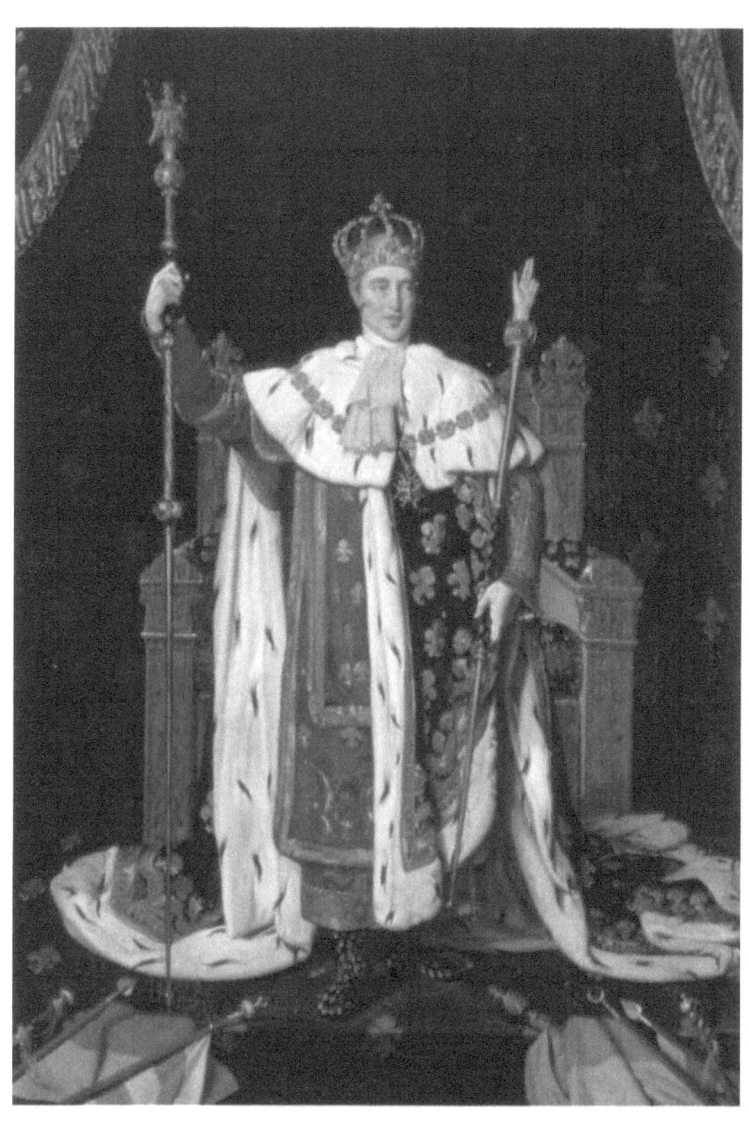

Portrait of Charles X in Coronation Robes, 1829
oil on canvas

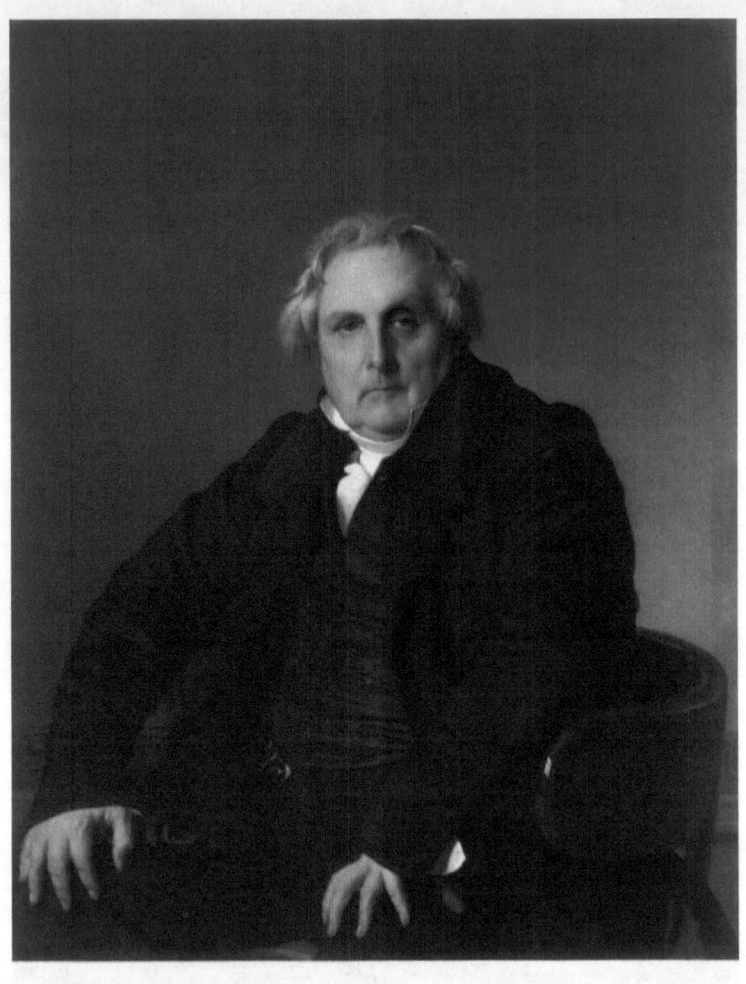

Portrait of French journalist Louis-François Bertin, 1832, oil on canvas

In portrait painting Ingres surpassed all his contemporaries. He could combine realistic exactitude with psychological insight, but still remain the sober observer, not involved in the inner life of his subjects. He could paint old men with the same supreme ease as young princesses, and capture the critical eyes of fellow painters as exactly as the dignity of political office, as in the portrait of Louis-Fran3ois Bertin (1766-1841), one of the leading personalities between the July monarchy and the Second Empire. He established the Journal des Dйbats which supported the policy of Louis-Philippe.

As a portrait painter, Ingres has often been compared to Holbein, and in portraiture particularly the severity of line and exactitude of detail so typical of Neoclassicism often lend the subject a touch of special historical dignity.

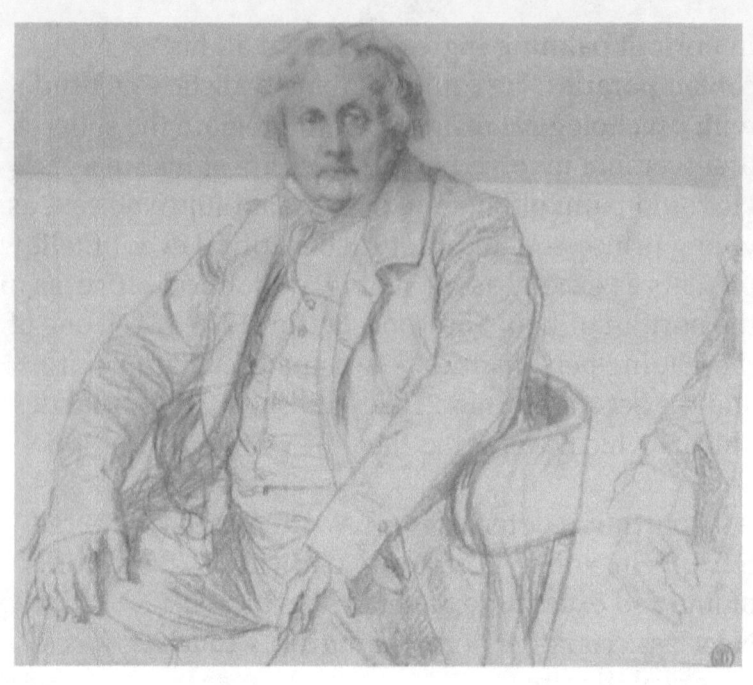

Study for the Portrait of Louis-François Bertin

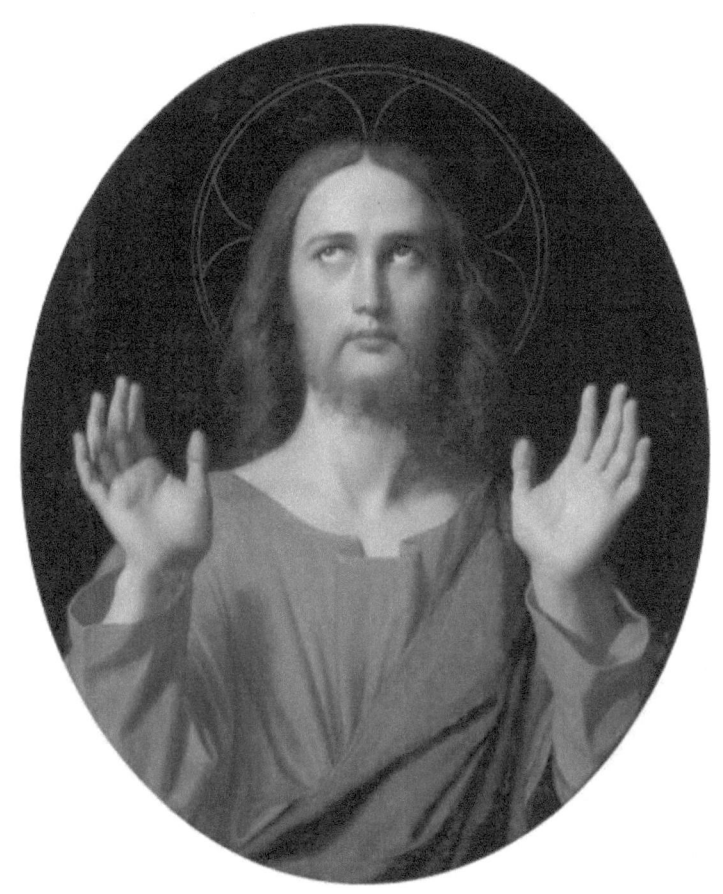

Christ, 1834, oil on canvas

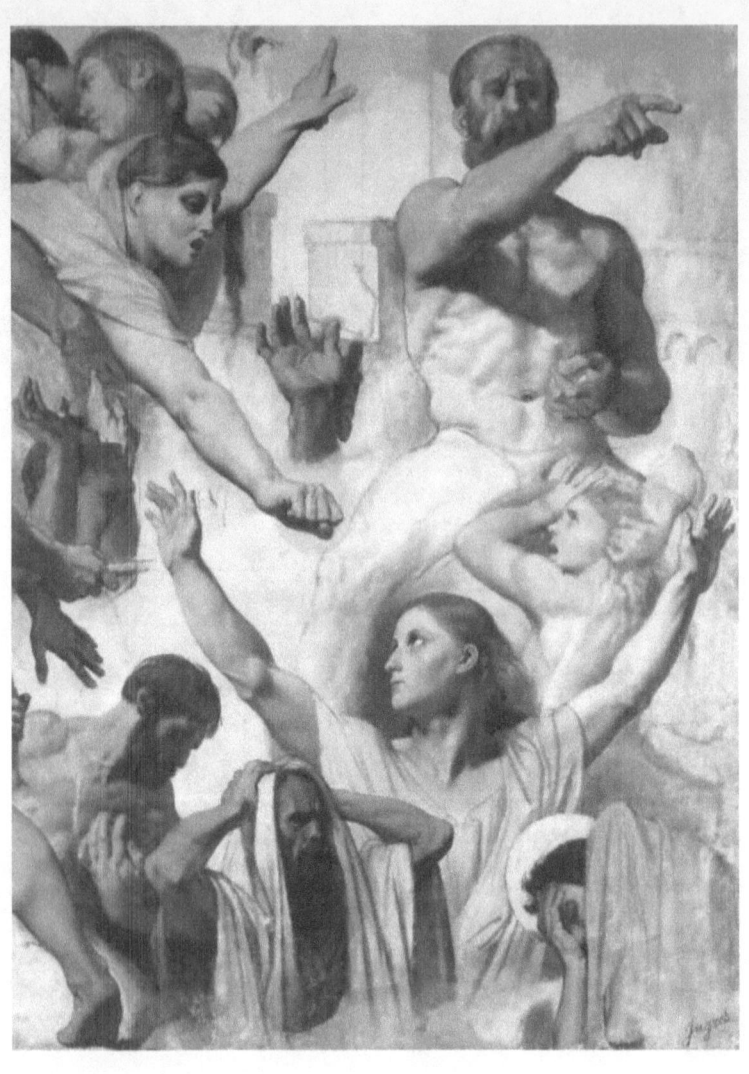

Study for The Martyrdom of St. Symphorien, 1824-1834, oil on canvas

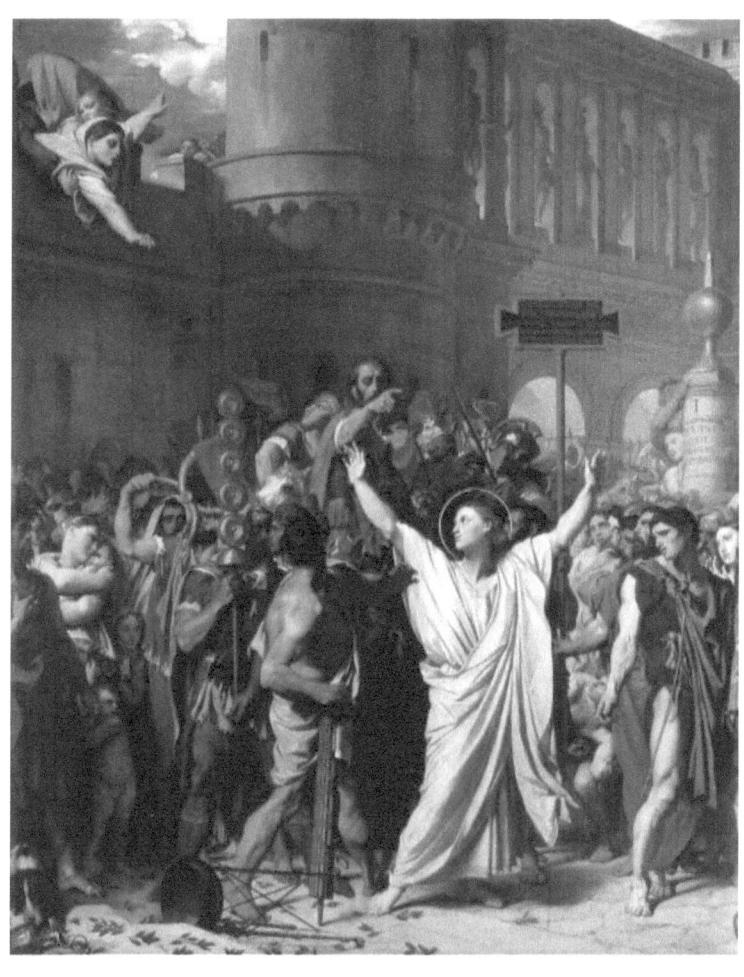

The Martyrdom of St. Symphorian, 1834, oil on canvas

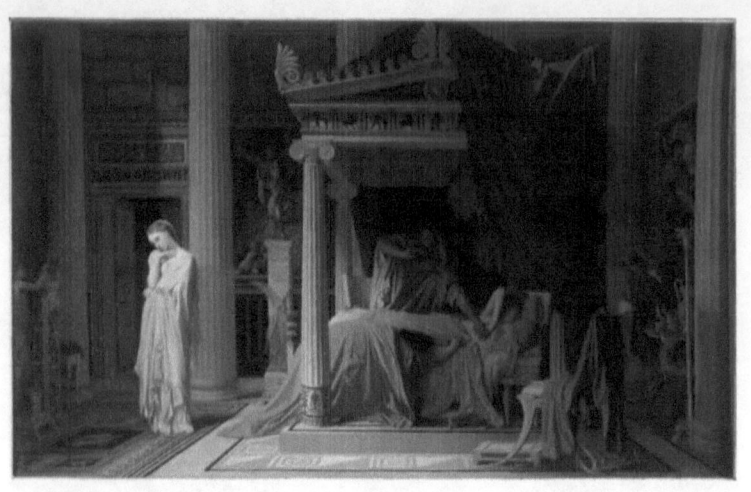

Antiochus and Stratonice, 1840, oil on canvas

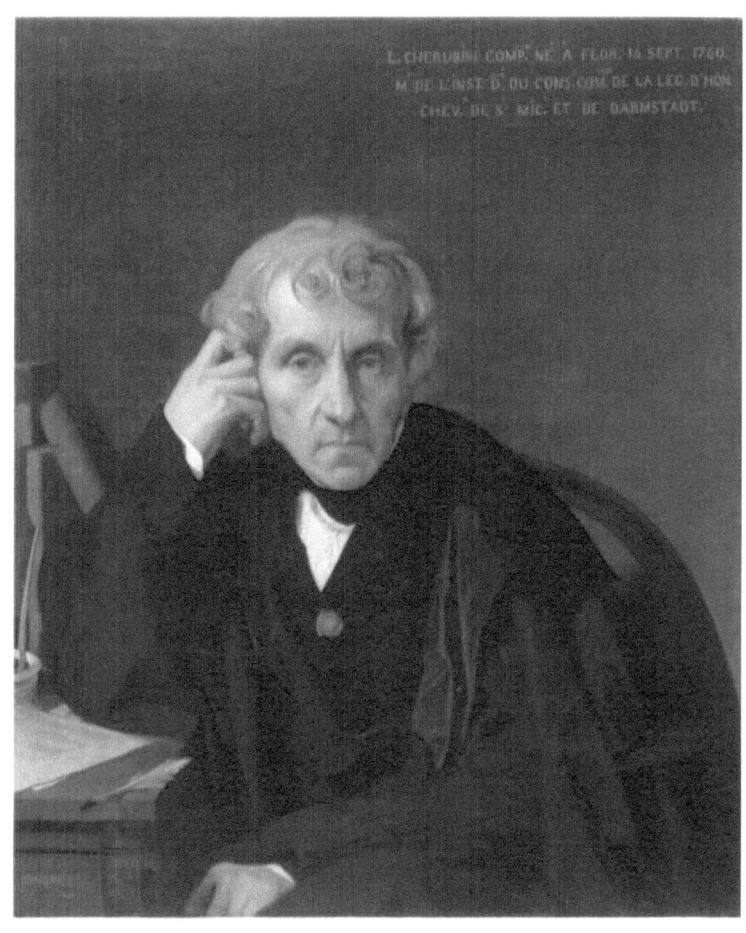

Luigi Cherubini, 1841, oil on canvas

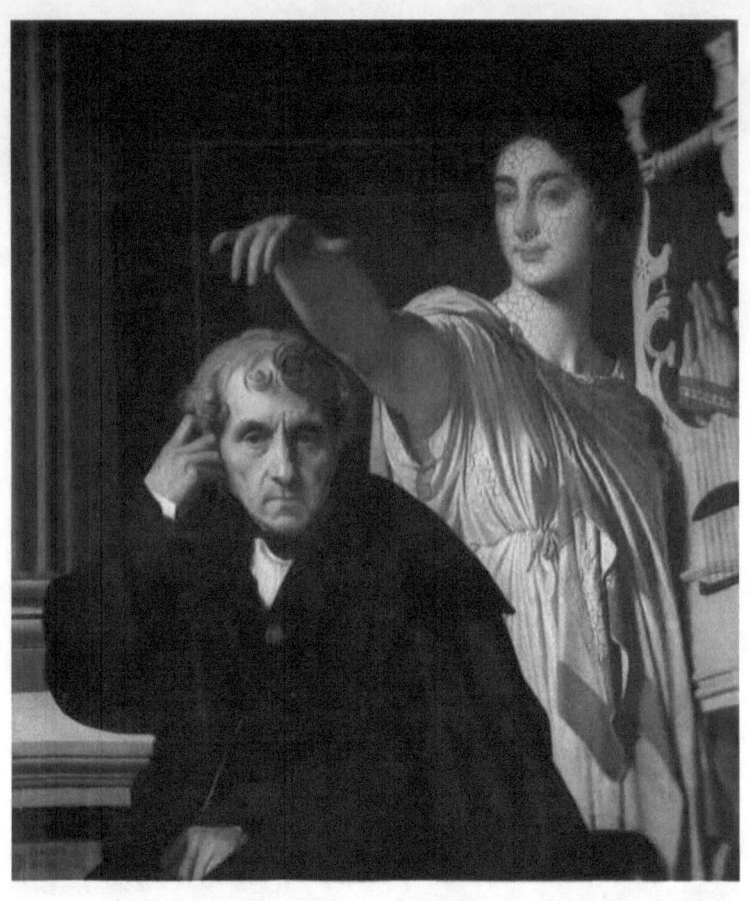

Luigi Cherubini and the Muse of Lyric Poetry, 1842, oil
on canvas

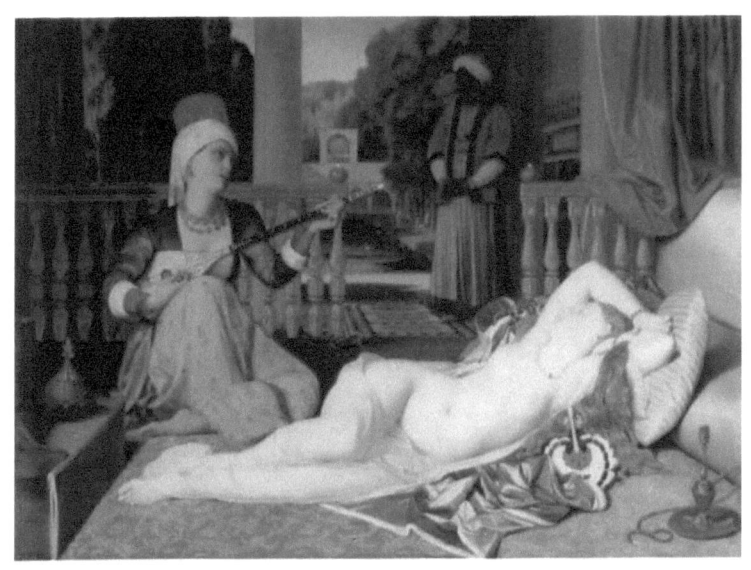

Odalisque with Slave, 1842, oil on canvas

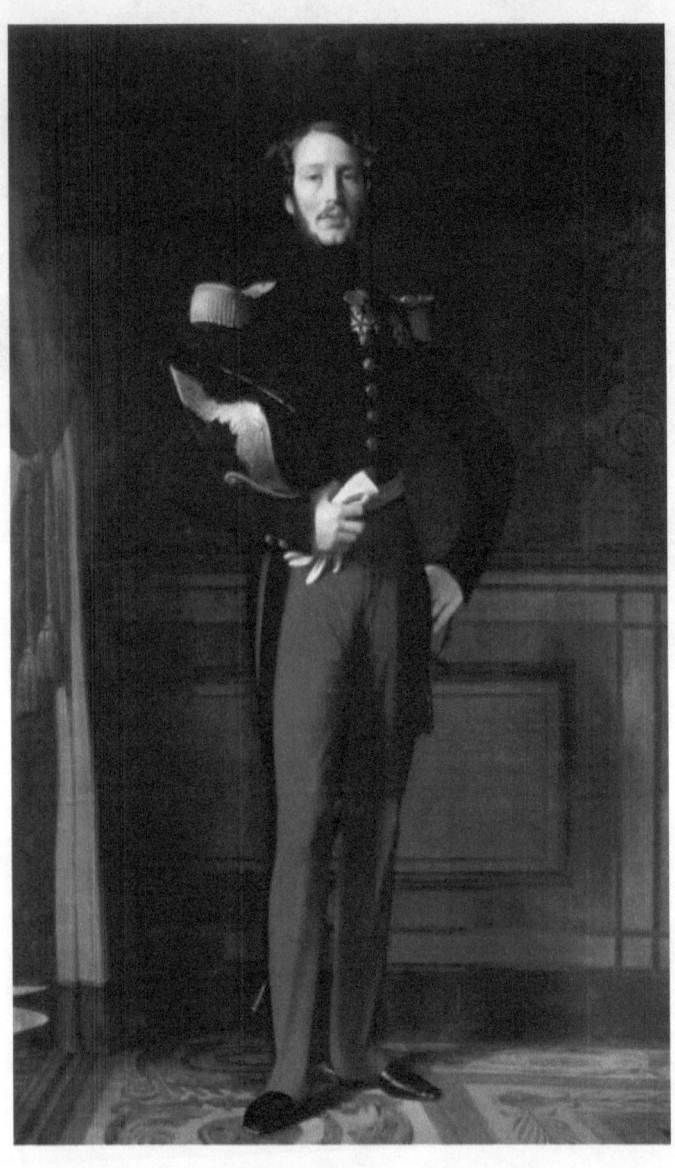

Portrait of Ferdinand-Philippe, Duke of Orleans, 1842,
oil on canvas

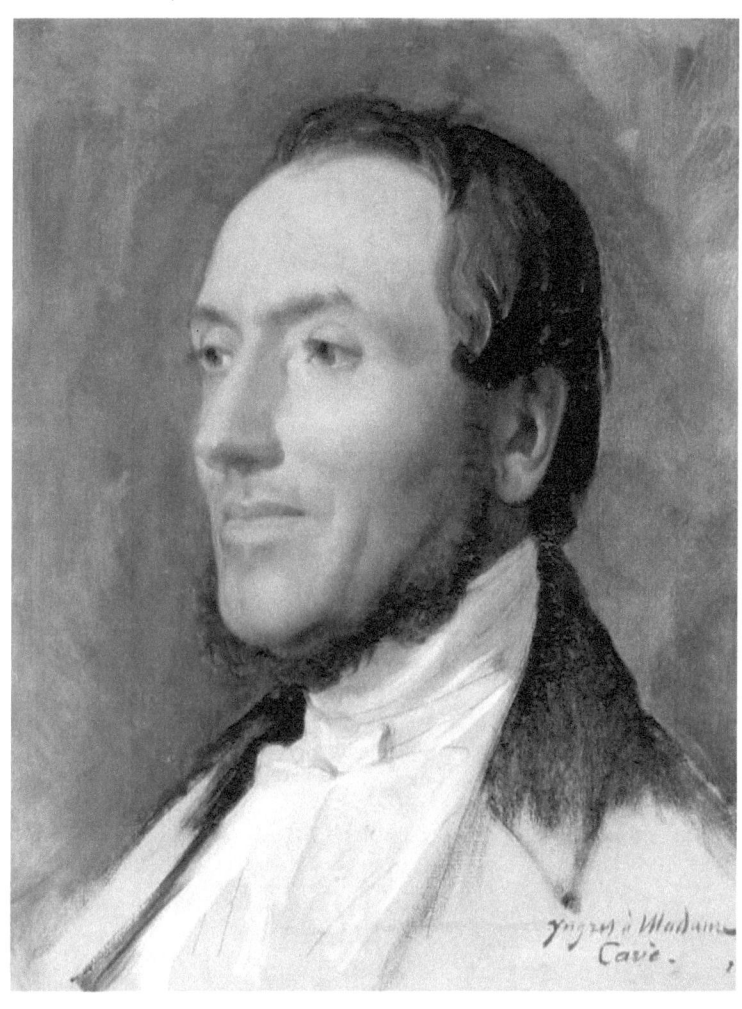

Hygin-Edmond-Ludovic-Auguste Cave, 1844, oil on canvas

Cavé held the high-ranking posts of inspector and director of the fine arts administration during the reign of King Louis-Philippe. Ingres painted this portrait soon after Cavé's marriage in 1844 to Marie-Elisabeth Blavot Boulanger.

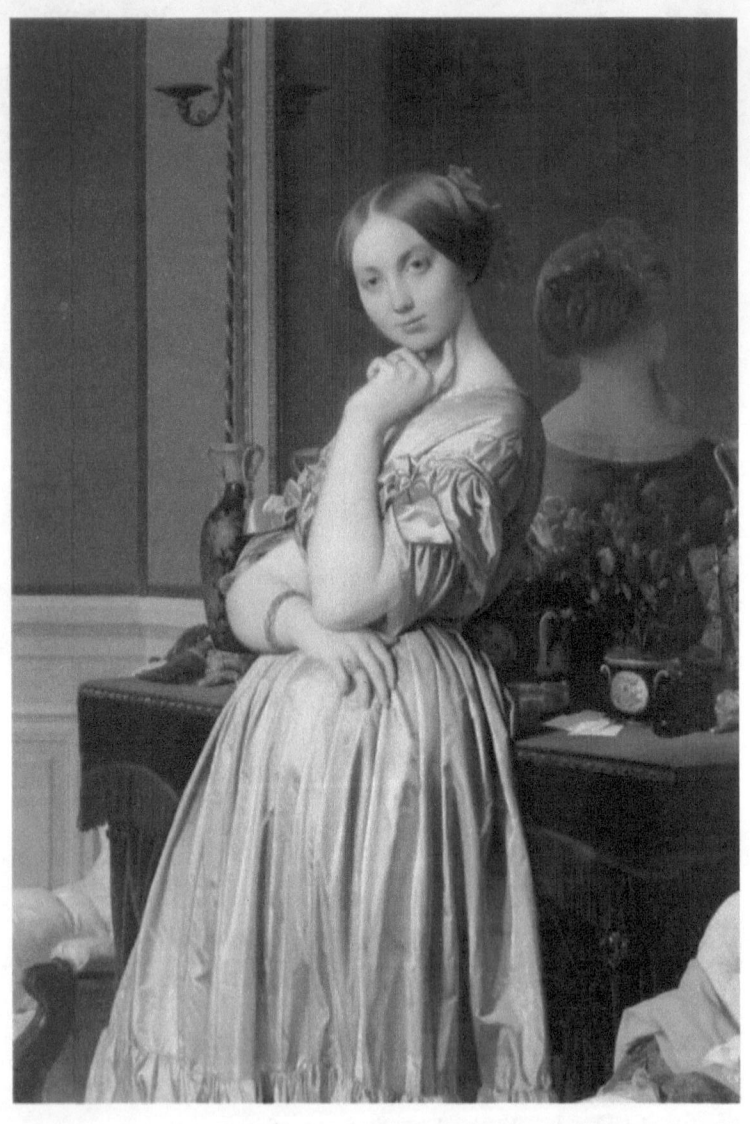

Portrait of Countess D'Haussonville, 1845, oil on canvas

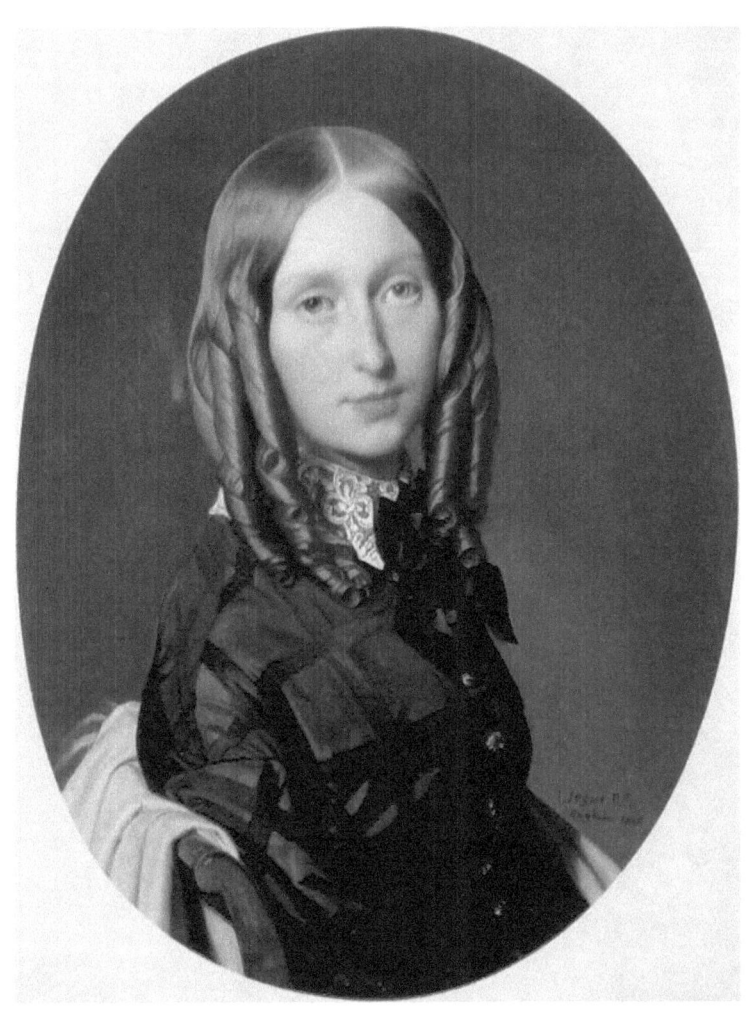

Portrait of Madame Frederic Reiset, 1846-1847, oil on canvas

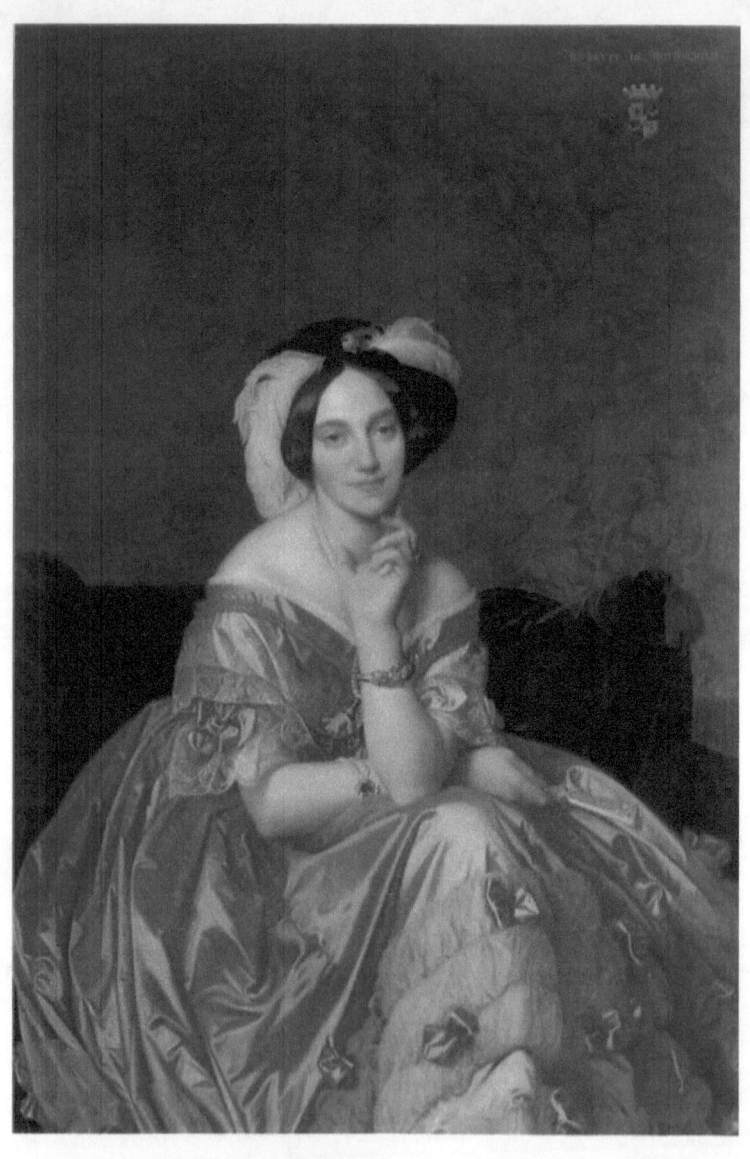

Baronesss Betty de Rothschild, 1848, oil on canvas

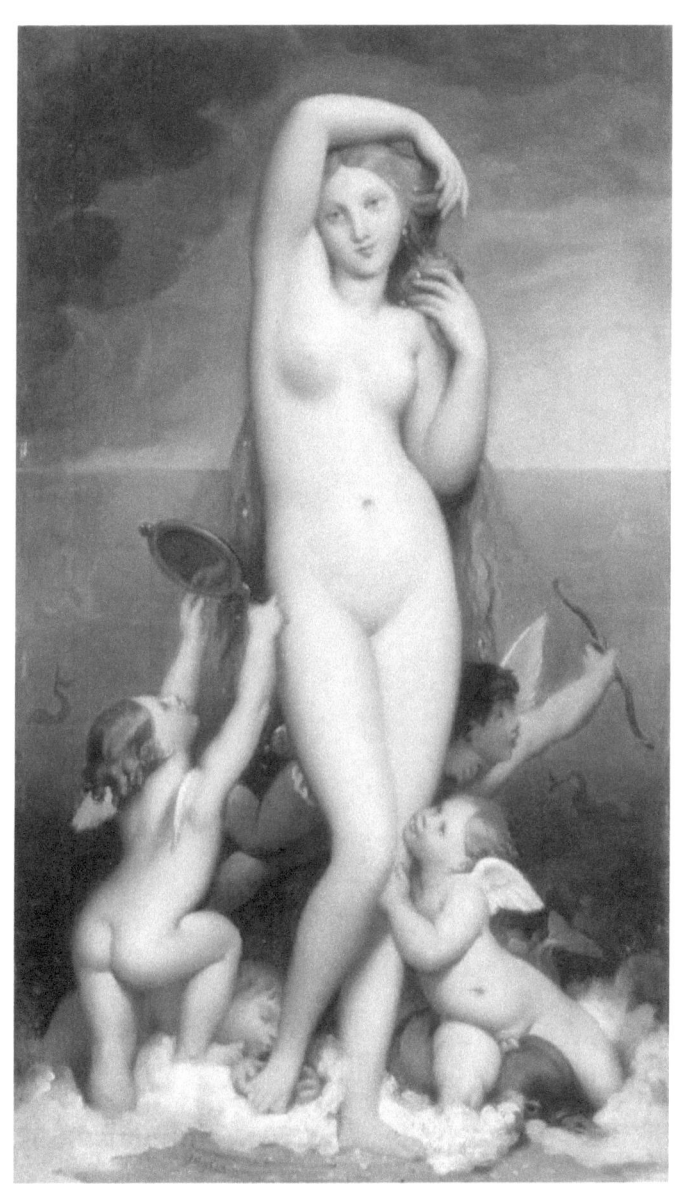

Venus Anadyomene, 1848, oil on canvas

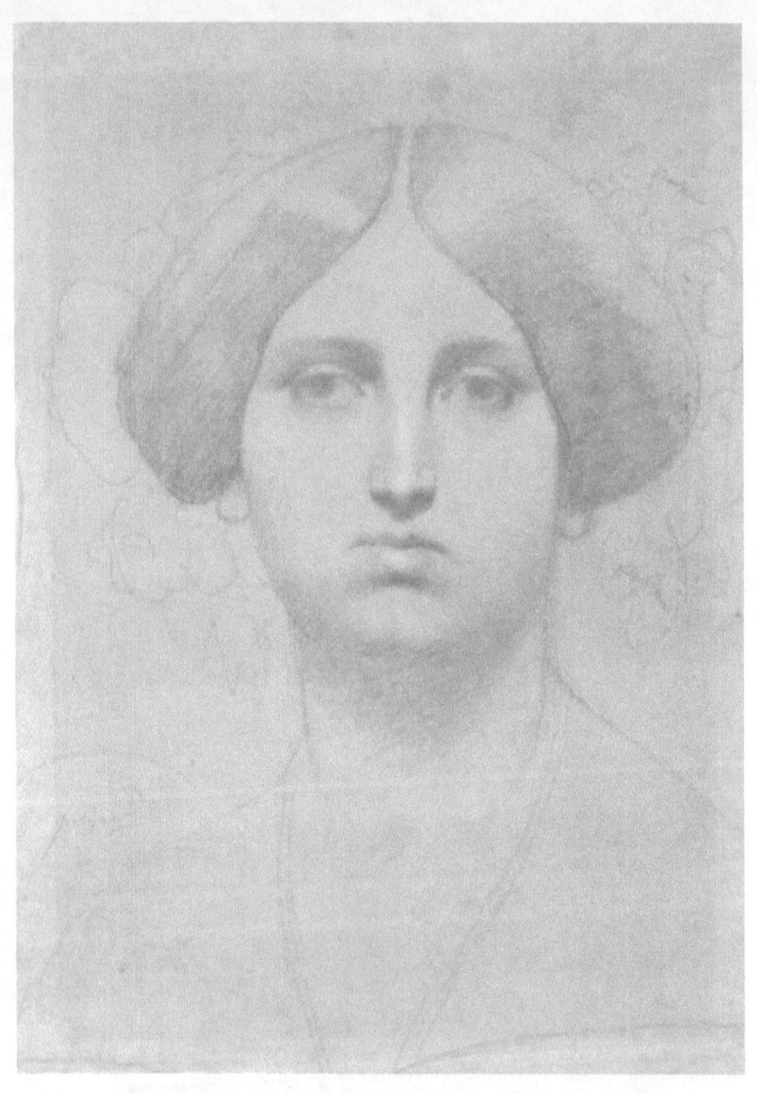

Study of Madame Moitessier, 1851, Graphite and white
chalk
*"Never did beauty more regal, more magnificent, more
stately, and of a more Junoesque type, offer its proud lines to
the tremulous pencil of an artist."*

Thus wrote critic Théophile Gautier after watching Inès Moitessier pose for this portrait. Jean-Auguste-Dominique Ingres painted four oil portraits of her and made multiple drawings at many sittings. He made this drawing and six other preparatory studies for an early portrait.

Both a realist and a classicist, Ingres gave his sitter cool, idealized features recalling the smooth, balanced proportions of ancient marble sculpture. In contrast to the detail of her expressionless face, he broadly indicated the hair's abstract shape and lightly sketched in the outlines of the surrounding flowers with reminder notes of appropriate colors.

Edgar Degas, a great admirer of Ingres, once owned this drawing.

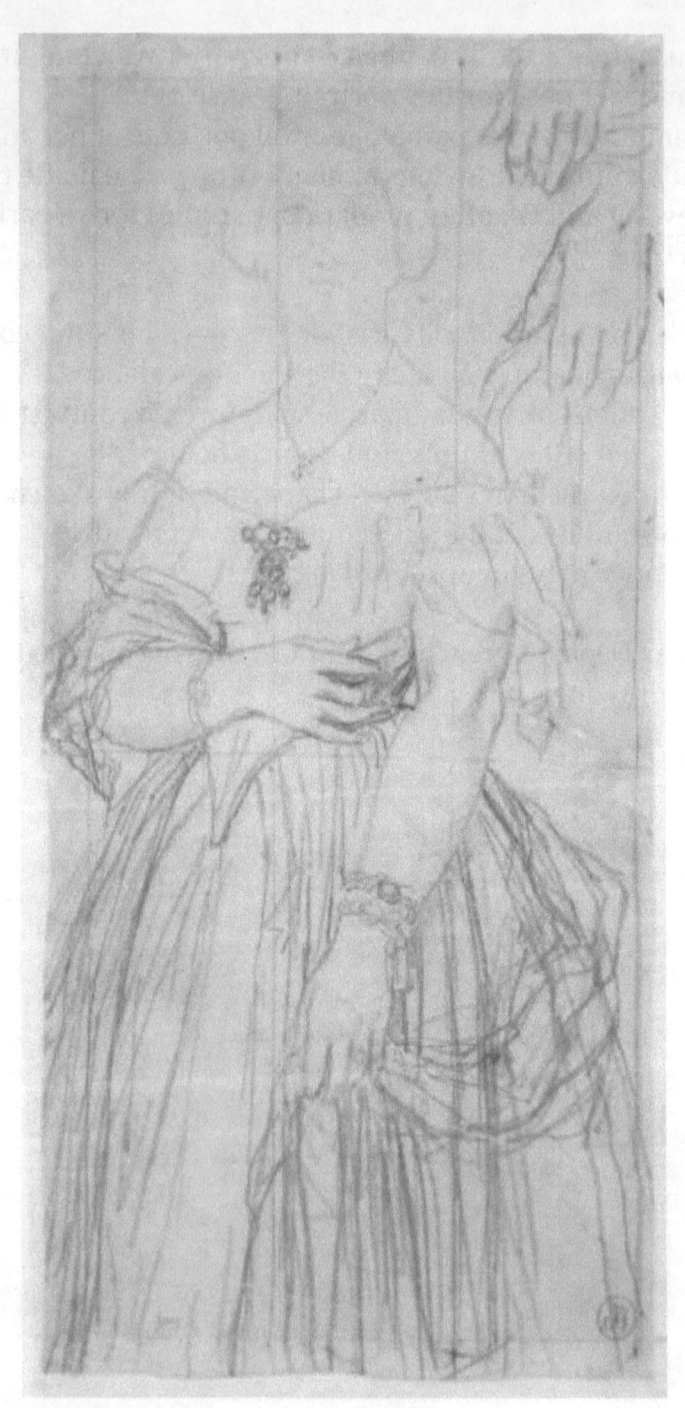

Study for the Dress and the Hands of Madame
Moitessier, 1851, Graphite on tracing paper, squared in
black chalk

In the crook of her right arm, Madame Moitessier
supports a loose, lacy shawl that twines around her.
Her brooch attracts attention while the tiny necklace
nearly disappears. In Jean-Auguste-Dominique Ingres's
later painting, a smaller brooch seems insignificant,
while a long string of pearls echoes the flowing sweep
of the woman's shawl and provides a purpose for the
hand at her waist. He made two additional studies of
her left hand in the upper right corner, exploring how
she might hold the shawl.

In this preparatory study for an 1851 painting, Ingres
concentrated on the woman's dress, her jewels, and the
positions of her arms and hands. To determine the
figure's proportions, he drew a grid or "squared" the
drawing. He freely worked out new ideas from the
bodice on down, probably tracing the head and
shoulders from another study. Ingres made many such
preparatory sketches for his four painted portraits of
Inès Moitessier, a banker's wife from a prominent
family of government officials.

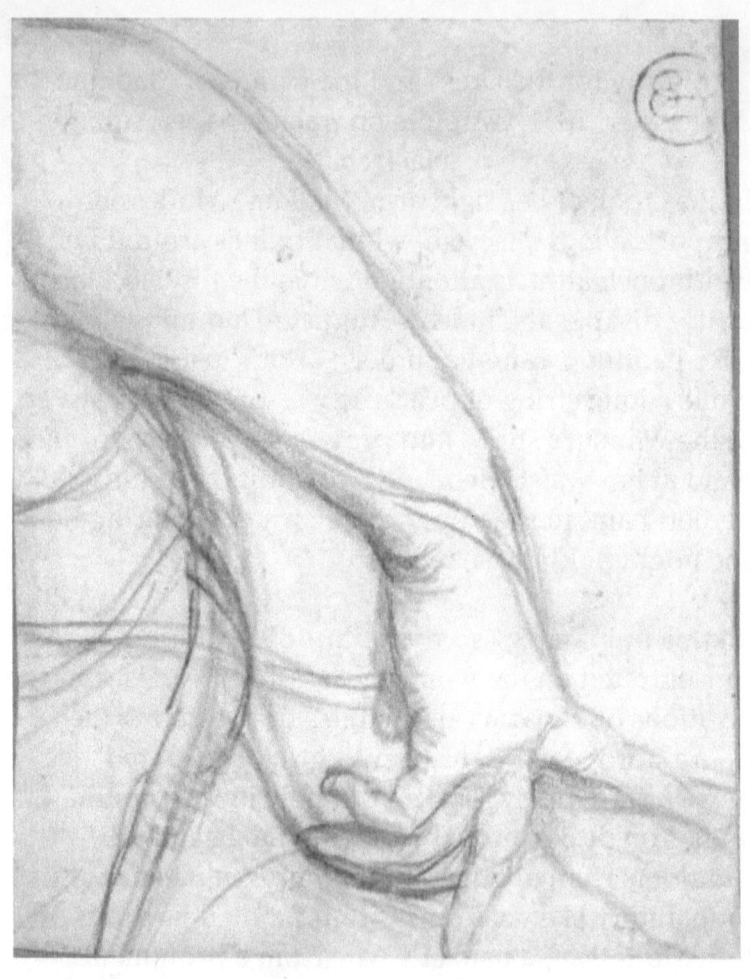

Study fo the right hand of Madame Moitessier, 1851,
Graphite on paper

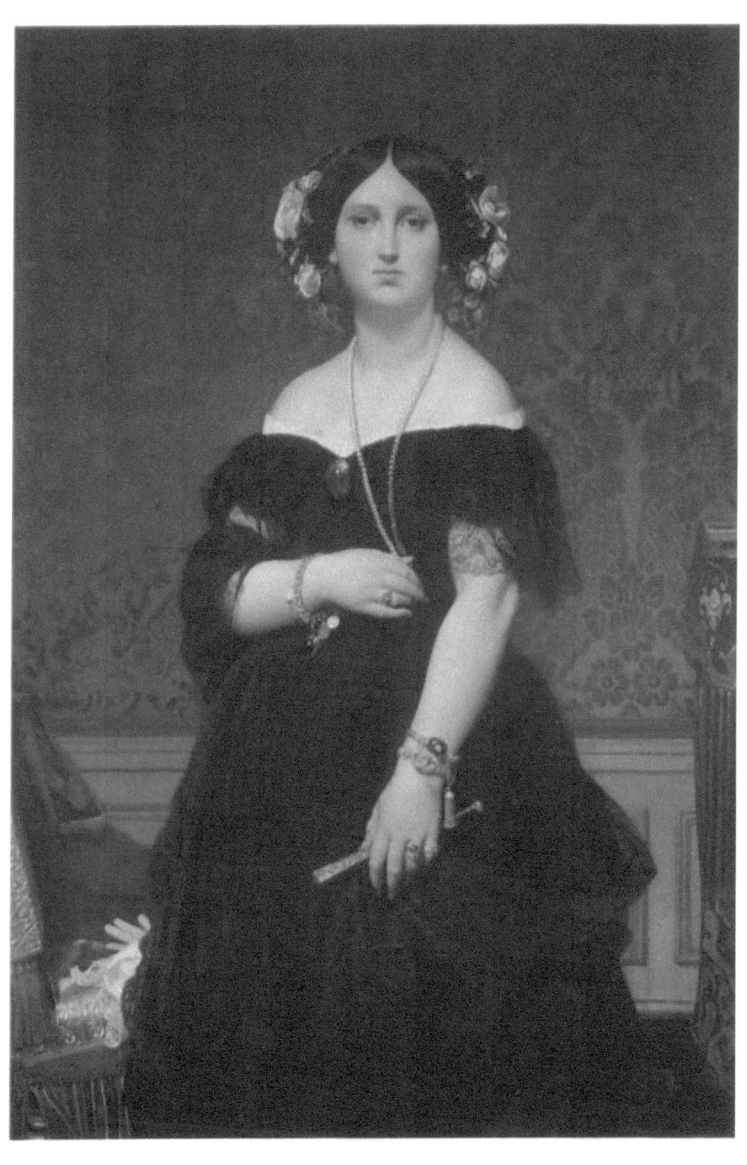

Portrait of Madame Moitessier Standing, 1851, oil on canvas

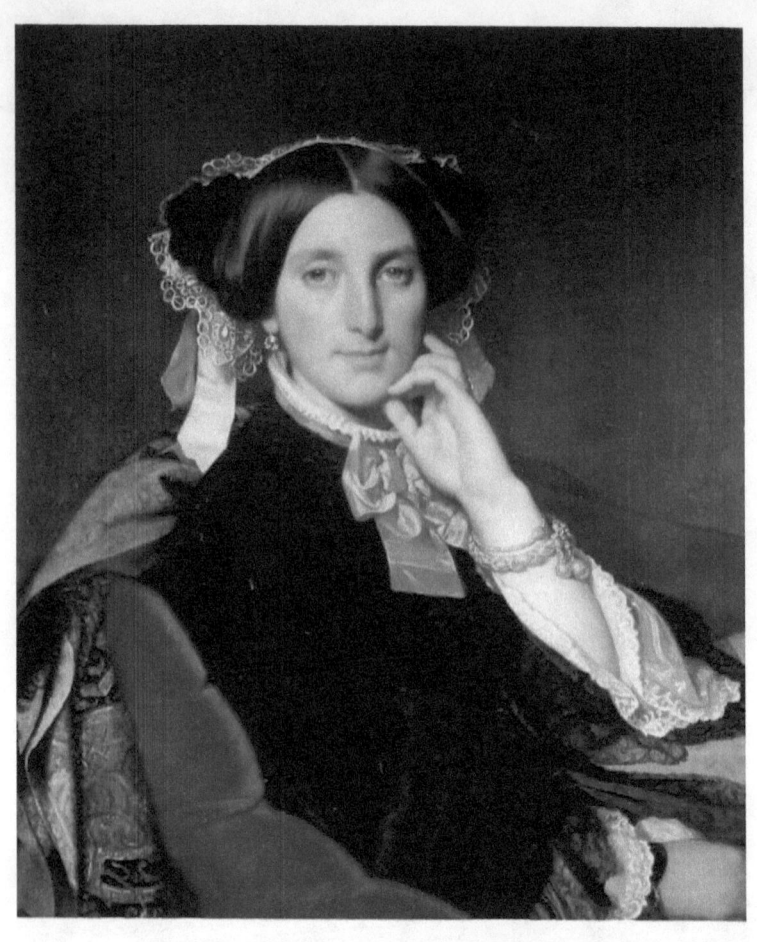

Madame Gonse, 1852, oil on canvas

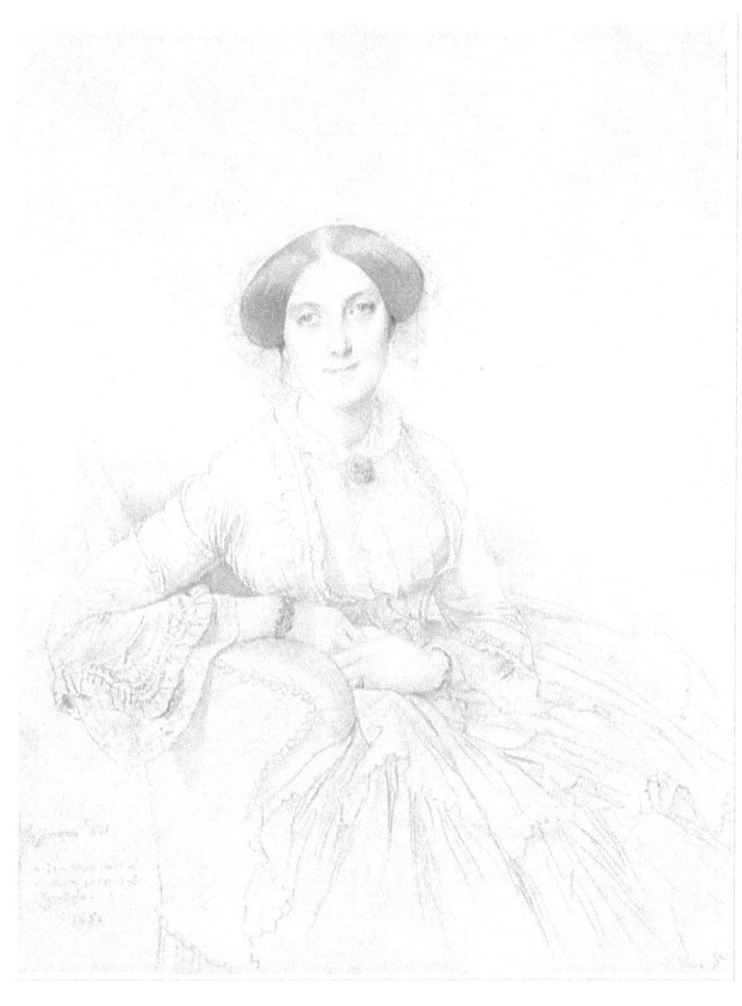

Madame Félix Gallois, 1852, Graphite with touches of
gold in oil to highlight jewelry, on buff wove paper

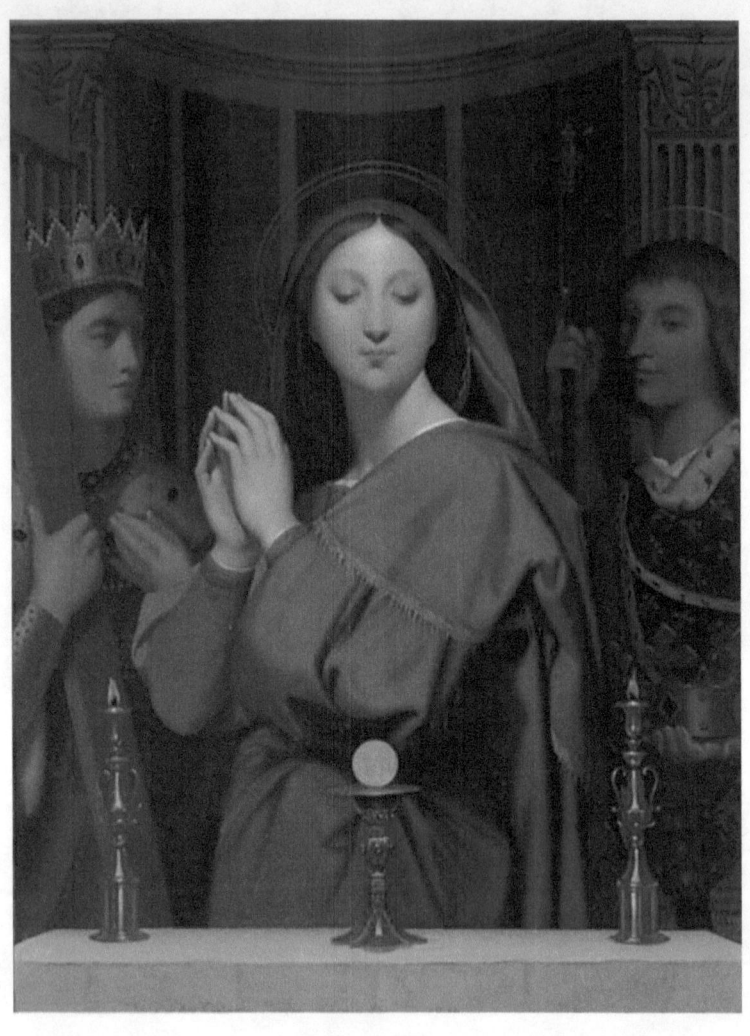

The Virgin Adoring the Host, 1852, oil on canvas

This small, jewel-like devotional painting was made as a gift for Ingres's friend Louise Marcotte, who introduced the artist to Delphine Ramel, whom he married in 1852. The Raphaelesque composition is based on one Ingres first painted in 1841 for the future czar Alexander II, which includes the two patron saints of Russia, Alexander Nevsky and Nicholas (Pushkin Museum of Fine Arts, Moscow). For this version, Ingres replaced the Russian saints with two French ones. He would go on to paint four more variants, as well as, in 1855, a watercolor for Madame Ingres herself.

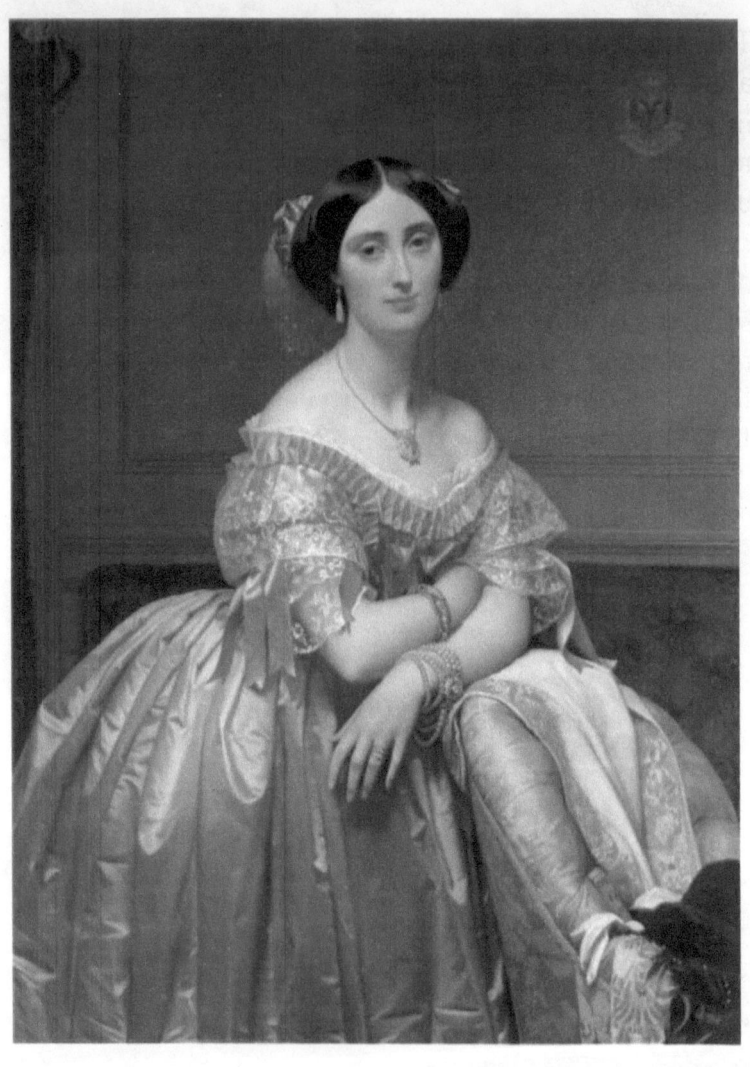

Portrait of the Princesse de Broglie, 1853, oil on canvas

Ingres was Jacques-Louis David's most celebrated pupil. His severe classical style and his meticulous working procedure epitomized the academic tradition, which he defended vehemently against the French Romantic movement, led by Eugɒne Delacroix. As a young man, he supported himself almost exclusively with commissioned portraits, but later in his life he hoped to renounce them for "grander things." Nevertheless, the last series of aristocratic portraits he made, between 1845 and 1853, were among the greatest achievements of his maturity.

The princesse de Broglie (1825-1860) was a great beauty and a highly respected woman, the embodiment of the best of the Second Empire aristocracy. Ingres began her portrait in 1851; after accepting the commission he wrote to a friend that it would be his last except for that of his wife. The painting completes his series of aristocratic portraits and is a supreme example of the mastery of technique, the bold use of colour, and the understanding of female character for which Ingres is so justly celebrated.

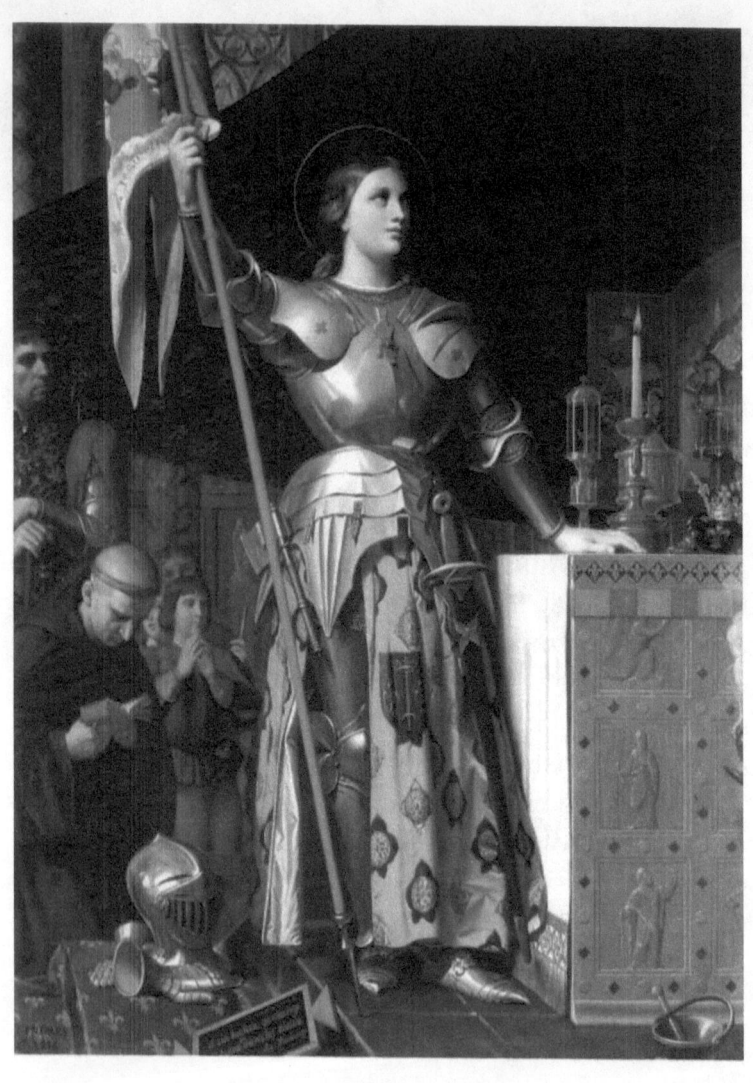

Joan of Arc on Corronation of Charles VII in the
Cathedral of Reims, 1854, oil on canvas

Charles VII (1403-1461) was a monarch of the House of Valois who ruled as King of France from 1422 to his death. In 1422, Charles VII inherited the throne of France under desperate circumstances. Forces of the Kingdom of England and the Duchy of Burgundy occupied Guyenne and northern France, including Paris, the most populous city, and Reims, the city in which the French kings were traditionally crowned. His political and military position improved dramatically with the emergence of Joan of Arc as a spiritual leader in France. Joan and other charismatic military leaders led French troops to several important victories that paved the way for the coronation of Charles VII in 1429 at Reims Cathedral.

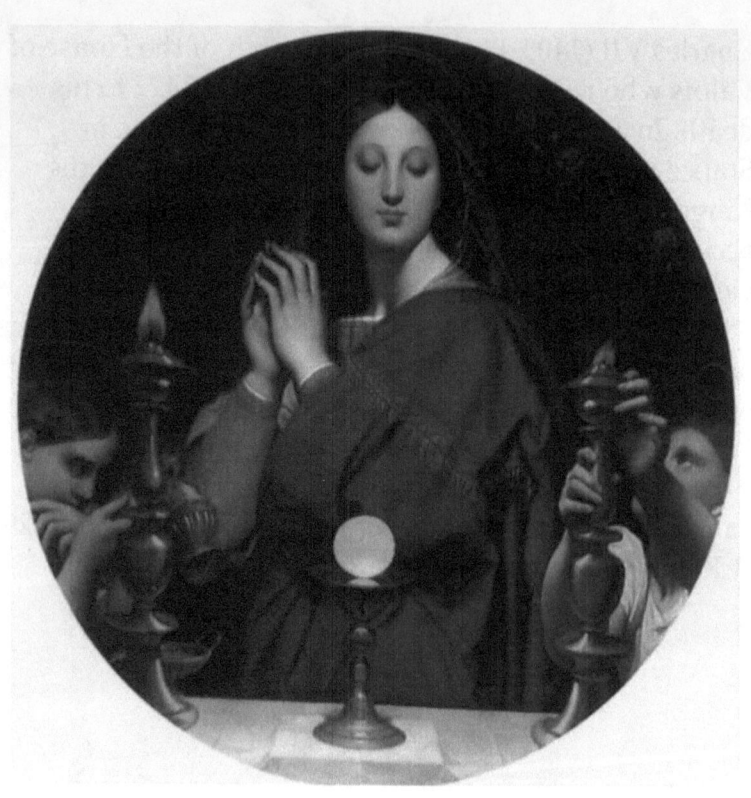

The Virgin of the Host, 1854, oil on canvas

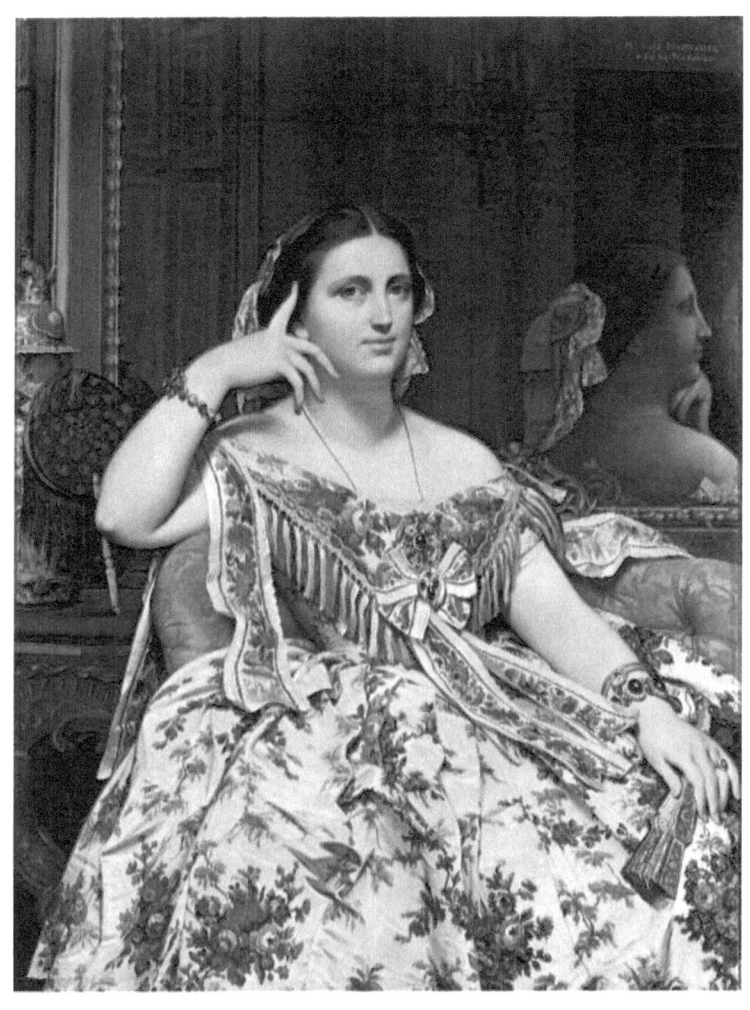

Madame Moitessier, 1856, Oil on canvas, 120 x 92 cm

It is often said that while Delacroix was the great proponent of French Romanticism, his older contemporary Ingres was the champion of the classical tradition: obsessed with Raphael and antiquity, upholder of 'drawing' versus 'colour'. Real life being less tidy, however, we find that Delacroix was a more calculating artist than the hyper-emotional Ingres, who did not hesitate to break academic rules for expressive ends. Both painted subjects from literature and history, and his response to the female nude is as charged with erotic longing and scarcely sublimated violence as Delacroix's. Nor did Ingres invariably emulate Raphael and Poussin. Throughout his long career he tried to match style to subject, looking in turn to Greek vase painting, to the Early Renaissance, even to the Dutch seventeenth-century painters of everyday life.

It is, however, true that drawing was of primary importance to him. Forced to support himself and his wife in Rome in 1814 by drawing the English tourists who flocked back to the city liberated from French rule, he developed a wonderfully spare, yet lively and descriptive line. Although he despised portraiture as a lower form of art, like his teacher David Ingres came to excel in it. Few of his painted portraits are more sumptuous than Madame Moitessier, begun in 1847 but completed only in 1856 when the artist, as he tells us in his signature, was 76.

He had originally refused to paint this wealthy banker's wife, but when he met her he was so captivated by her beauty that he agreed, asking her to bring her small daughter, 'la charmante Catherine', whose head is visible under her mother's arm in a preparatory drawing in the Ingres Museum in Montauban. The doubtless bored and wriggling child was soon banished as Ingres wrestled with the picture, requiring long hours of immobility from his model. The sitter's dress was changed more than once. Ingres is recorded as still working on the portrait in 1847. The death of his wife in 1849 left him in despair and unable to paint for many months. In 1851 he began sittings anew and completed a standing likeness of Inas Moitessier in black (now in Washington). He returned to the seated version in 1852.

When he had finished four years later the sitter was 35. Ageless like a goddess with her Grecian profile impossibly reflected in a mirror parallel to the back of her head but dressed with Second Empire opulence in flowered chintz, Madame Moitessier exemplifies the ambiguities of Ingres's art. The firm contour of her shoulders, arms and face defines flesh perfectly rounded - though barely modelled - and as poreless, smooth and luminous as polished alabaster, yet paradoxically soft to the touch. In contrast to the resiliently buxom horsehair settee, it arouses fantasies and fears of bruising. The pose, with head resting against the right forefinger, derives from an ancient wall painting and signifies as Ingres must have known matronly modesty. But 'classicising' devices are offset by the minutely realistic transcription of the surfaces of fabrics, the fashionable parure of jewels, ormolu frames, Oriental porcelain. The mixture of the general with the particular, timeless grandeur with bourgeois ostentation, languor with pictorial rigour, is unique to Ingres and far from bloodlessly Neo-classical.

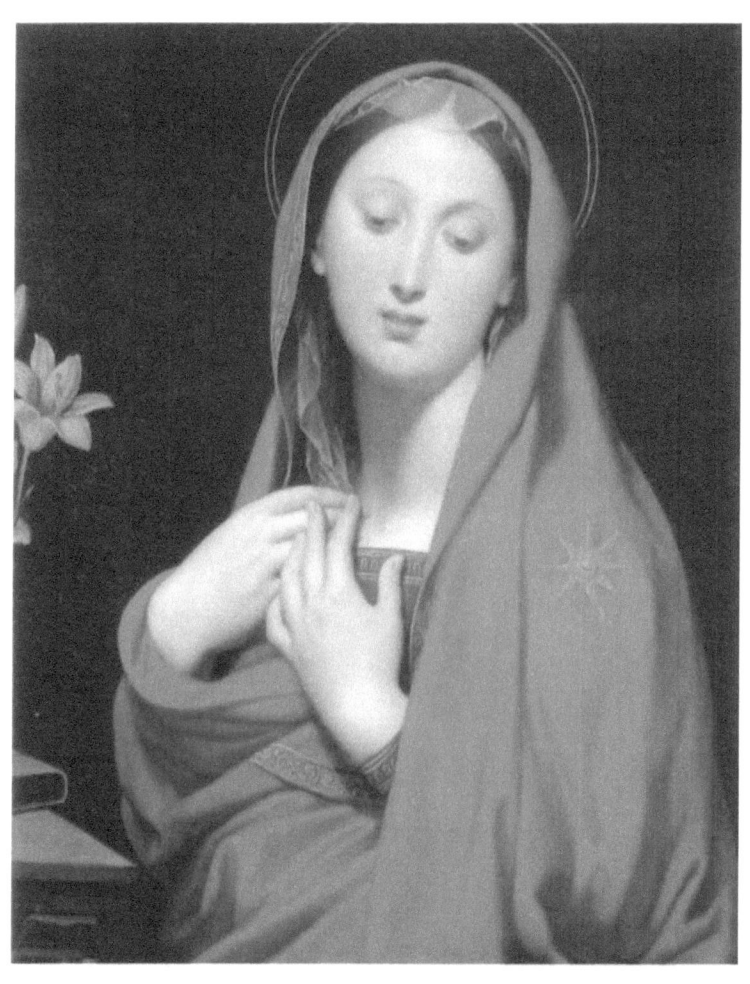

Virgin of the Adoption, 1858, oil on canvas

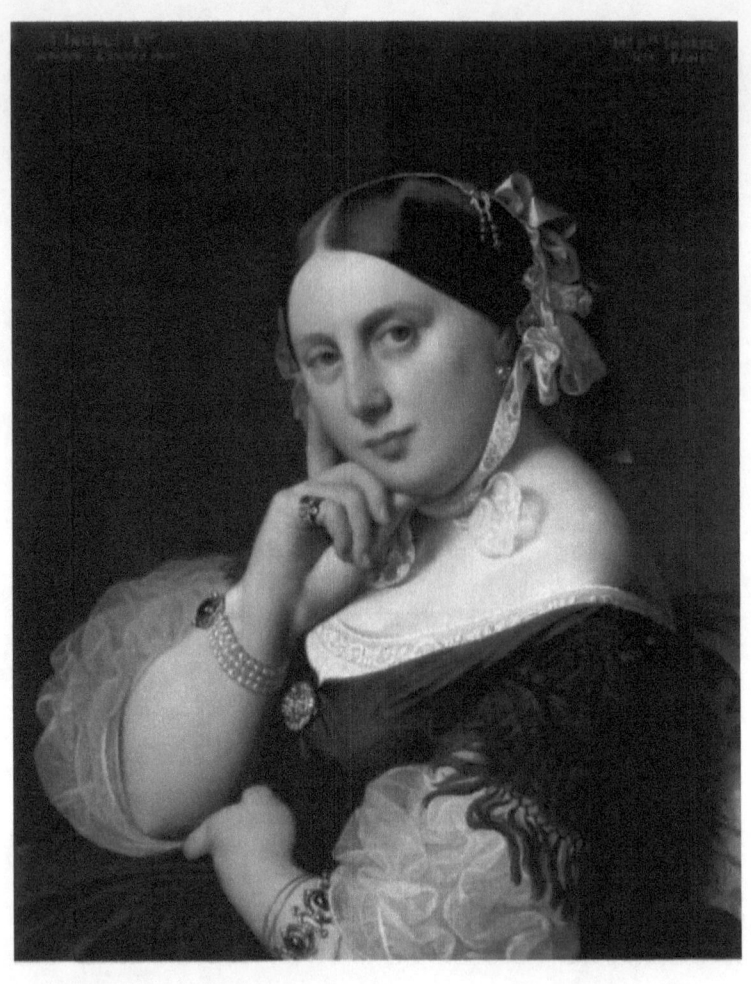

Delphine Ramel, Madame Ingres, 1859, oil on canvas

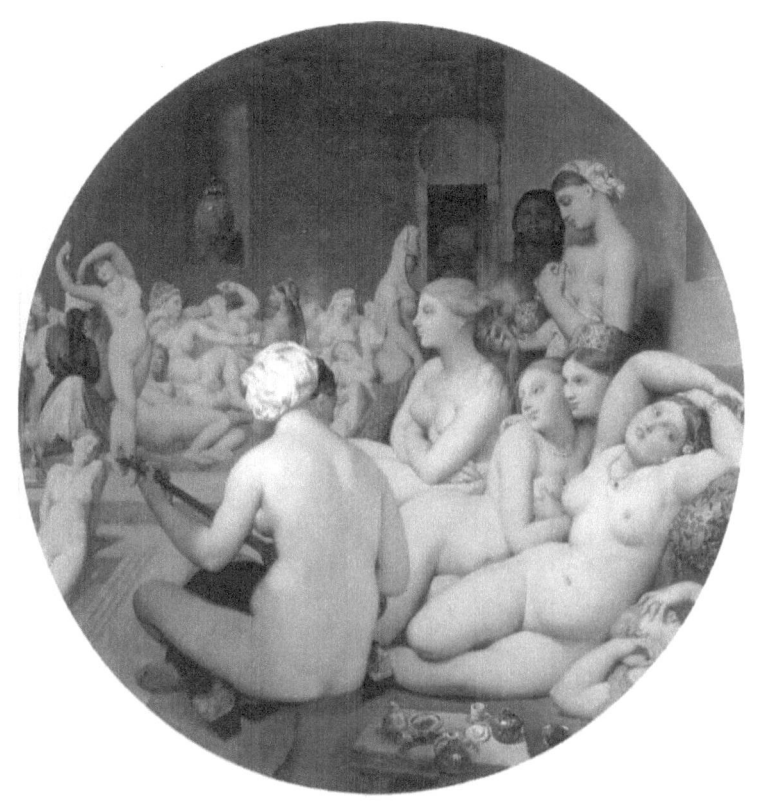

The Turkish Bath, 1863, oil on canvas
Ingres derived the idea of these swarming nudes in the
interior of a harem from Lady Mary Wortley
Montague's letters. She was the wife of the English
ambassador to the Sublime Porte; in these two letters
she describes baths in the Seraglio, which she was
allowed to enter, and Ingres copied extracts from them
into his notebook, probably in about 1817.

Several of the figures in this canvas have been taken from earlier pictures; others are new. Ingres had not a very ready imagination, and borrowed from both French and English prints of 'turqueries', going back to the eighteenth or even the sixteenth centuries. Copies of these are still to be seen in the archives of his studio in the Musñe de Montauban.

This picture has existed in at least two forms. A first sketch, intended for Comte Demidoff, was executed in 1852, but not delivered; it was probably worked on again after this date, and at the end of 1859 it was bought by Prince Napoleon. The appearance of this picture, which at that time was square, is known from a photograph dated 7 October 1859. On the intervention of Princess Clotilde, scandalized by all those nudes, the Prince returned it to Ingres; M. Reiset was entrusted with negotiating its exchange for a portrait of the artist at the age of twenty-four (now in the Musñe Condñ, Chantilly). Ingres kept the picture for several years, making various changes in it and giving it its final circular form. He signed it in 1862, indicating with pride that it was the work of a man of eighty-two.

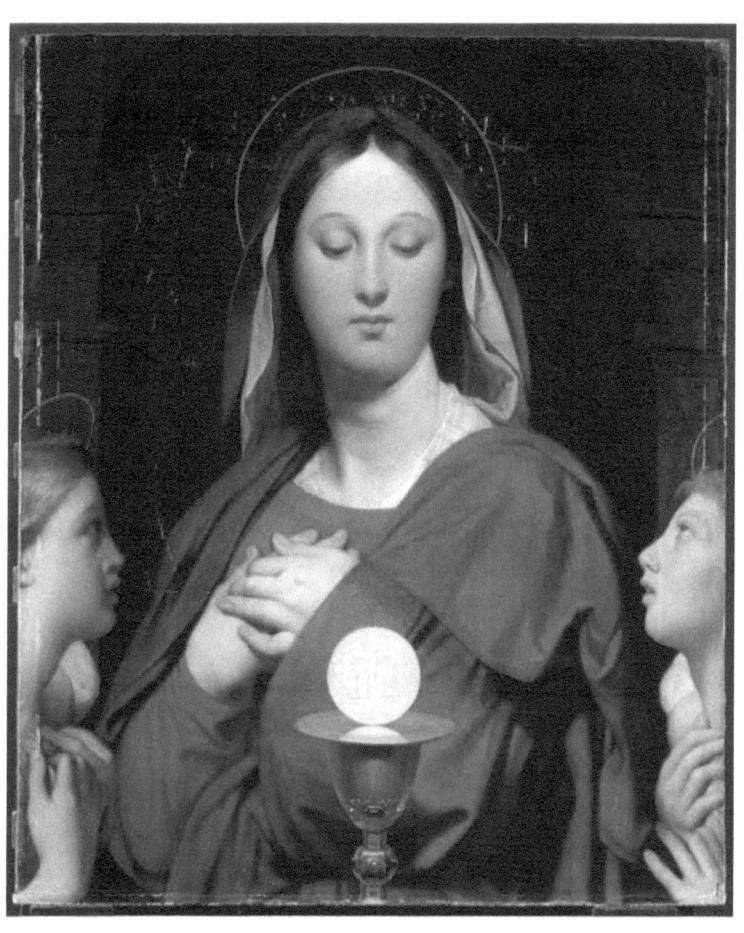

The Virgin of the Host, 1866, oil on canvas

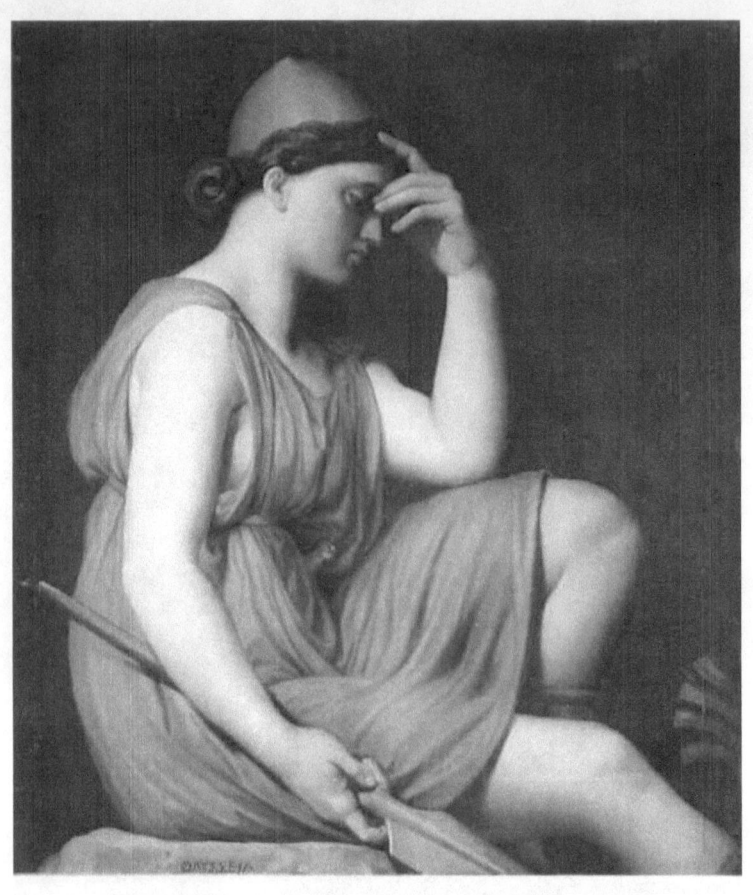

Odysseus, Study for the Triumph of Homer, oil on
canvas

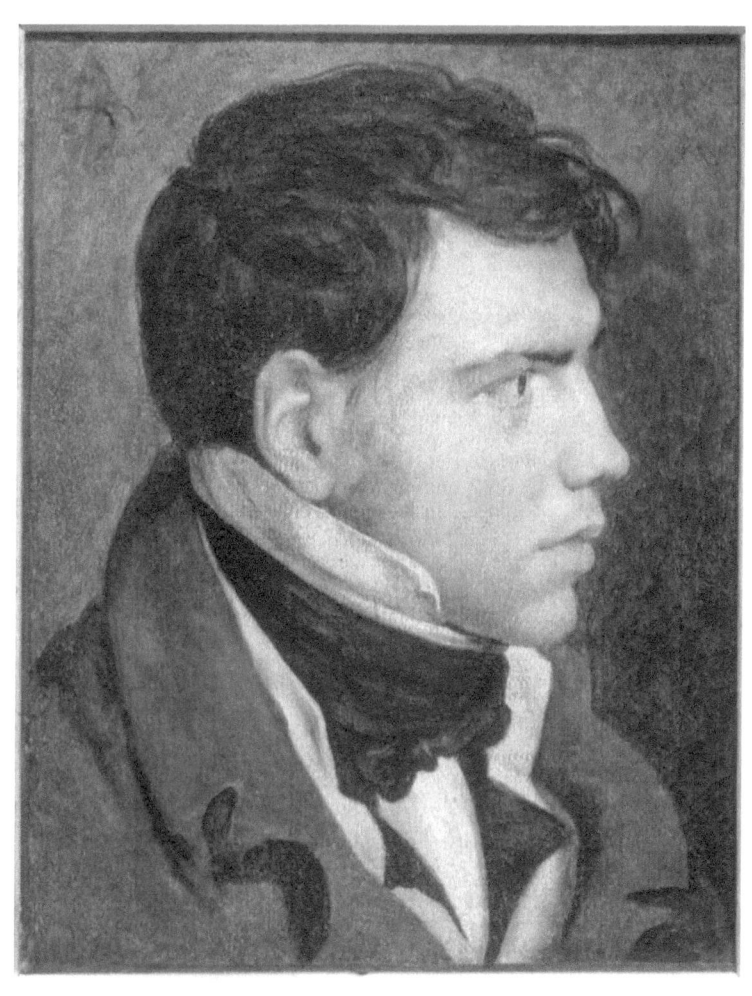

Portrait of a young man, oil on canvas

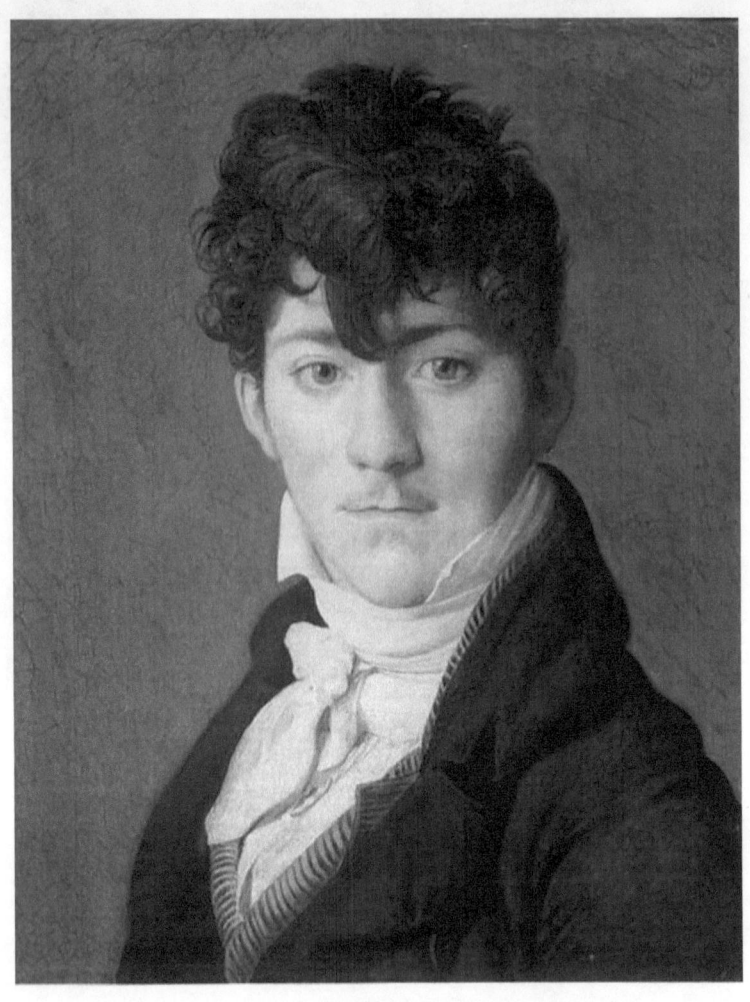

Portrait of Auguste Francois Talma, Ensign, nephew of
the tragedian Talma, oil on canvas

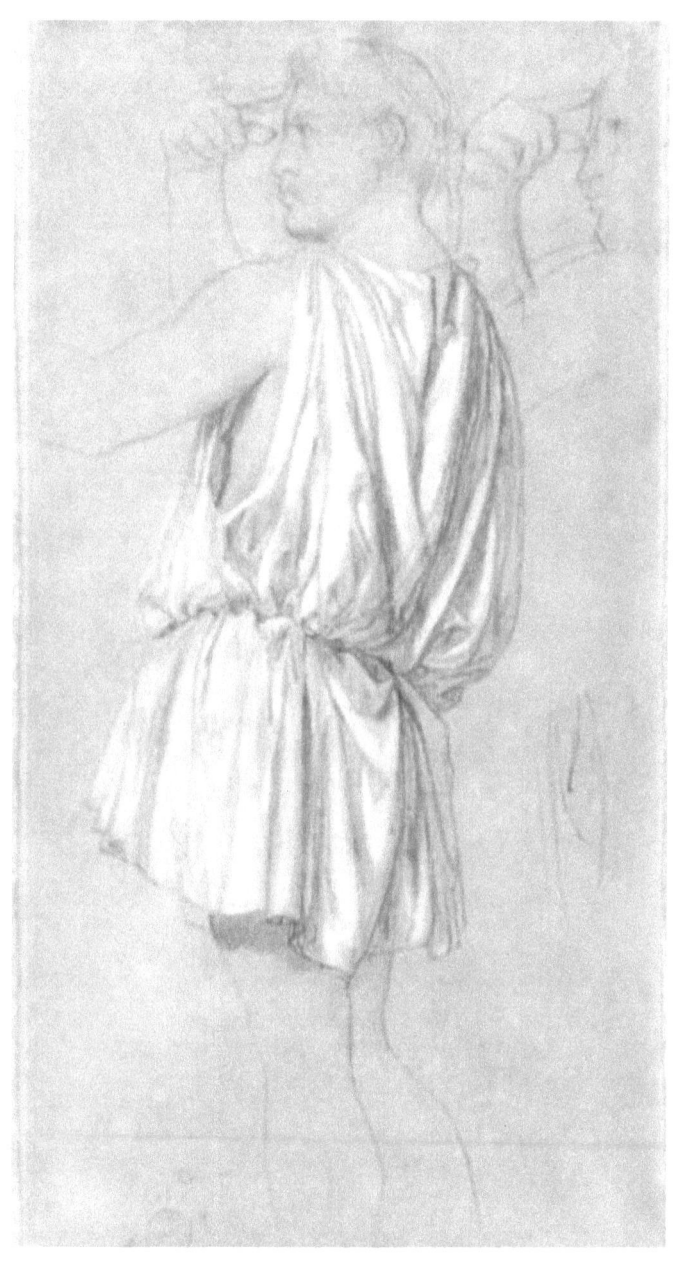

Study for the figure of Phidias in 'The Apotheosis of Homer', graphite and bodycolour on buff paper

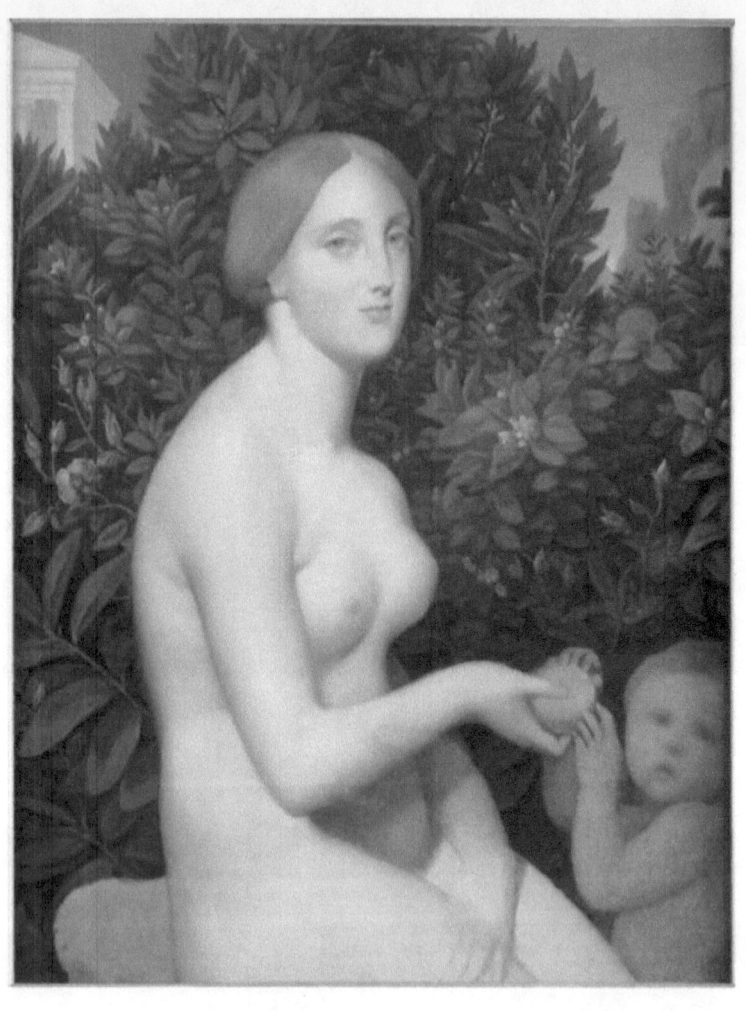

Venus at Paphos, oil on canvas

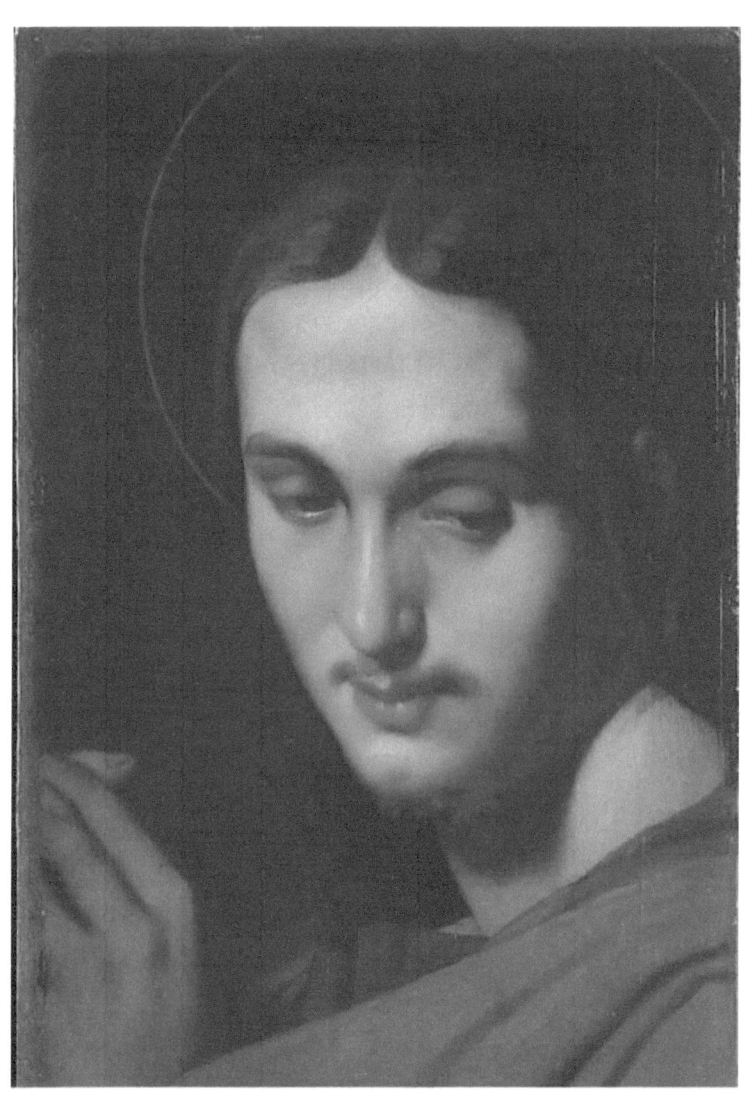

Head of Saint John the Evangelist, oil on canvas

This is a study for an altarpiece, Christ Delivering the Keys to Saint Peter, commissioned in 1817 for Santissima Trinità dei Monti, Rome, and completed in 1820 (now Musée Ingres, Montauban). Ingres based the composition on Raphael's tapestry design of the same theme and developed it in eight oil studies (including this one) and more than seventy drawings. Although the study may date to 1818–20, it is also possible that it was painted or reworked in 1841, and touches may have added as late as 1856.

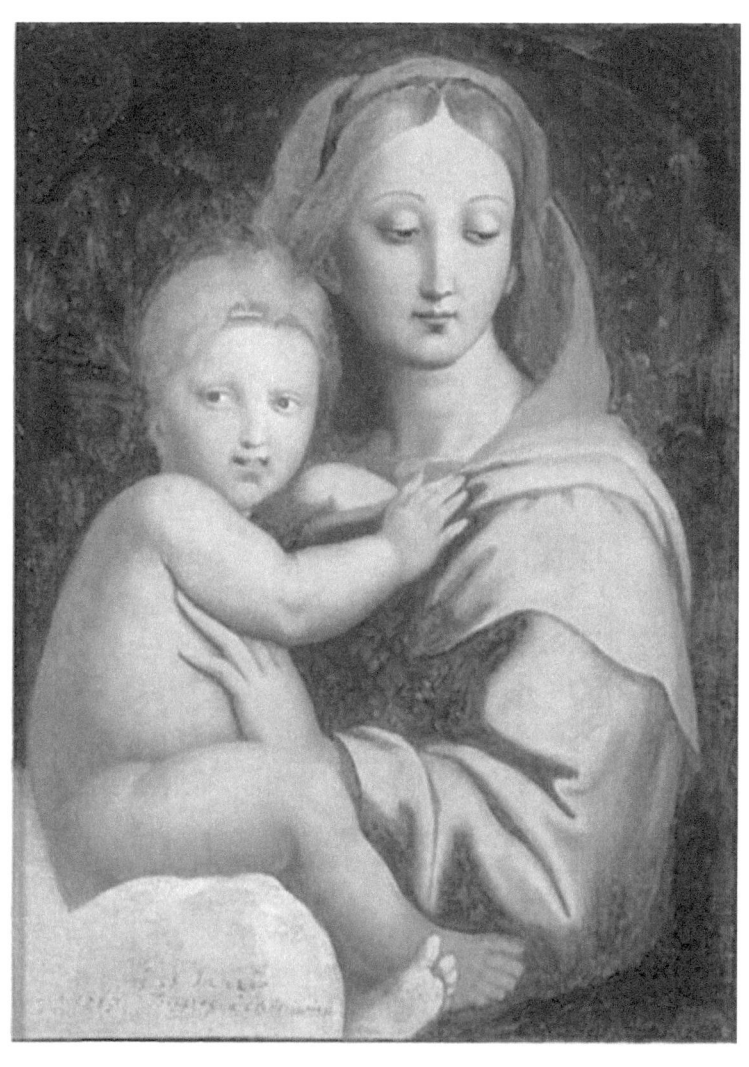

Virgin and Child with candelabra, oil on canvas

www.ingramcontent.com/pod-product-compliance
Lightning Source LLC
Chambersburg PA
CBHW020918180526
45163CB00007B/2789